This book is dedicated to
the men and women of the
private security industry
in South Africa

ABOUT THE AUTHOR

Doraval Govender is Professor in the Department of Criminology and Security Management at the University of South Africa, where he is the Academic Head of the programme: Security Management. Spanning 42 years, his career in security has included work in many areas of policing, with a major portion of his career spent in criminal investigations. He served in the South African Police Service as Assistant Commissioner (Major General). His qualifications include: PhD in Criminology (Security management), MTech in Forensic Investigations, BA Honours in Security, BA Honours in Public Governance, BA in Policing, and National Diploma in Education Training and Development.

MANAGING
SECURITY
INFORMATION

INCIDENTS, THREATS and VULNERABILITIES

A practical approach for security practitioners
serving private and government entities in South Africa

Doraval Govender

UNISA PRESS
PRETORIA

© 2018 University of South Africa
First edition, first impression

Print ISBN 978-1-86888-910-5
e-ISBN 978-1-77615-000-7

Published by University of South Africa Press
University of South Africa
P O Box 392, 0003 University of South Africa

Prior to acceptance for publication by University of South Africa Press, this work was subjected to a double-blind peer review process mediated through the Senate Publications Committee of the University of South Africa.

Editor: Ruth Botman
Indexer: Elsabé Nell
Design & typesetting: Unisa Press
Cover design: Luba Qabaka

Telephone: 086 12 DALRO (from within South Africa); +27 (0)11-712-8000
Telefax: +27 (0)11-712-8374
Postal Address: P O Box 31627, Braamfontein, 2017, South Africa
www.dalro.co.za

Readers are advised that the points of view expressed and practices recommended within this work are those of the author, and do not necessarily represent the official position or policies of any law enforcement agency or academic institution.

Contents

Illustrations

Table

Figures

Acronyms

ATM	automated teller machine
ASIAL	Australian Security Industry Association Liaison
ASIOBLU	Australian Security Intelligence Organisation Business Liaison Unit
BAC	Business Against Crime
BIS	business intelligence system
CAG	Council of Australian Governments
CAS	crime administration system
CCF	Crime Combating Forum
CCTV	closed circuit television
CEO(s)	chief executive officer(s)
CGRI	Consumer Goods Risk Initiative
CGCSA	Consumer Goods Council of South Africa
CIAC	Crime Information Analysis Centre
CIMC	Crime Information Management Centre
CIOs	crime information officers
CISF	Critical Infrastructure Security Forum
CIT	cash-in-transit
COB	computerised occurrence book
Compstat	The "Compare statistics" program, a management tool for police departments
CPA	crime pattern analysis
CPF(s)	community police forum(s)
CPTED	crime prevention through environmental design
CTA	crime threat assessment
DSRM	Department of Security Risk Management
ECU	Edith Cowan University
GIS	geographic identification system
GISS	Global Information Security Survey
ICT	information and communication technology
IRIS	incident reporting information systems
ISCTISN	industry security committee and trusted information sharing networks
IMS	incident management system

IPA	incident pattern analysis
JOCOM	joint operational committee
MANCOM	management committee
MISS	minimum information security standards
MOU	memorandum of understanding
NDPP	National Directorate of Public Prosecutions
NICOC	National Intelligence Coordinating Committee
NIM	National Intelligence Model
NPA	National Prosecuting Authority
OHS	occupational health and safety
PPS	physical protection systems
PSI	Petroleum Security Initiative
PSIRA	Private Security Industry Regulatory Authority
SABRIC	South African Banking Risk Information Centre
SAICB	South African Insurance Crime Bureau
SAPRA	South African Petroleum Retailers Association
SAPS	South African Police Service
SASOL	South African Synthetic Oils and Liquids
SIA	Security Industry Alliance
SIAU	security information analysis unit
SIMM	security information management model
SIU	Special Investigations Unit
SMS	short message system
SRMC	security risk management cycle
SRMM	security risk management model
SOPs	standard operating procedures
SWOT	strengths, weaknesses and opportunities
TSA	Technikon South Africa
TA	threat assessment
UNISA	University of South Africa
UK	United Kingdom
US/USA	United States (of America)
VA	vulnerability assessment
WA	Western Australia
WAP	Western Australian Police

Foreword

by David Dodge, CPP PCI FSyI MIS(SA)
Chairman, South African Institute of Security

South Africa's mineral wealth is known around the world, as is the diversity and richness of its cultures and the attraction of its major landmarks, including cities such as Cape Town and Johannesburg, both of which featured as 'major cities with the highest quality of life in the world' during a recent survey. These are some of the many drivers that attract over 10 million visitors to the shores annually.

Unfortunately, some see another side to life, and death, in South Africa, in terms of its crime rate – notably including over 50 murders a day according to the most recent crime statistics. This alone presents a mammoth task for the countries public and private security practitioners to identify, analyse and evaluate such rich data, or 'big data' as it is now known, to enable them to make meaningful interventions to protect life and property.

In this book, Professor Govender has identified the need for effective security information management, with the emphasis on the term information, as opposed to the often-misused term intelligence. Google Dictionary differentiates the two terms as: "Information – facts provided or learned about something or someone" and "Intelligence – the collection of information of military or political value." It goes without saying that information is considered the core ingredient of intelligence and so requires effective management and processing to be of real value.

Bringing attention to the need for a structured approach to information management, as an essential tool in the kitbag of all security professionals, Professor Govender's model is something to be applauded and highly recommended throughout both private and public sectors. If applied consistently and effectively, this must ultimately lead to an improvement in information-sharing between stakeholders and intelligence-led interventions to reduce incidents of crime and the effects of them.

The security information management model (SIMM) developed is based upon his extensive personal experience as a senior police officer in South Africa and leading academic with research across the globe. This research was most notably in South Africa and Australia, but has significant references to other models such as the USA's Compstat and UK's intelligence-led approach to policing and the National Intelligence Model (NIM), essentially information management systems that I am more familiar with as a retired London detective!

Having relocated to South Africa and moved into the private security sector, I have all too often heard people rave about a practice in such and such a country that they have tried to implement locally, only to see it fail to produce the expected results.

In developing the Model and the practical approach to security information management in South Africa, the author has avoided such a pitfall by considering approaches in a variety of contexts and then formulating that which is most appropriate in the local context.

In this book, Professor Govender has provided a detailed account of his research and developed a SIMM that can significantly improve the effectiveness of public and private security practitioners in South Africa.

Not only is this book a must read, but I believe the approach is a must do!

Foreword

by Anthony Minnaar
Research Professor in Criminal Justice Studies
University of South Africa

In this publication, Prof Doraval Govender has produced a comprehensive study focused on the management of security information by security practitioners in the field of private security. However, it is as applicable for security managers and risk managers working in government departments and entities.

In the process of researching this topic, Prof Govender also investigated aspects of the sub-discipline of security risk management. As a starting point for his analysis he used the broad concept/term 'security', which in itself implies that there exists the threat of risk. Such security risk or threat can emanate from a number of different quarters inter alia terrorism, cybercrime and other forms of criminality or identity/personal information theft threat. As a result, organisational management decisions on security risk control measures need to be taken in order to secure an organisation from all of these diverse threats. The security industry itself operates within a diverse and multi-disciplined knowledge base, with security risk management being a fundamental knowledge domain within the security environment.

Accordingly, his study was undertaken in order to understand the role of security information and its collection, interpretation and utilisation in addressing the threat of risks facing in the security industry and the clients they serve and protect. Any incidents of information theft, breaches in security, threats and vulnerabilities have the potential to negatively affect an organisation's assets. Therefore, as Prof Govender points out, information on these incidents, threats and vulnerabilities are crucially important to any organisation's overall security.

The core outcome of his research and outlined in detail in this book was the development of a security information management model (SIMM). In brief, this model is explained as follows: Security information management is spread out in three phases, namely the collection of security information phase; analysis of security information phase; and the implementation of security risk control measures phase. The collection and the analysis of the security information is handled by the Security Information Management Centre (SIMC) and referred to top management as an analysis report (result/outcome). The analysis report is handled by top management and referred to the operational manager or the human resources manager for the application of security risk control measures. This Model also serves to provide a platform for analysis of any incidents regarding breaches, loss or theft of an organisation's information, as well as assisting in the identifying of any shortcomings and/or existing vulnerabilities in terms of security information management in any organisation so that effective counter measures can be implemented to further secure and protect an organisation's information systems.

This publication is a valuable addition to the core body of knowledge for the 'young' discipline of Security Management and the sub-discipline Security Risk Management and is highly recommended reading for all security practitioners and security managers in the private and public sectors of the security industry and will hopefully assist in the further professionalisation of this core industry involved in the protection and safe keeping of all communities.

Acknowledgements

I wish to express my gratitude to a number of people and organisations, who have assisted me in thought and deed for the duration of the research and writing of this book.

- To SAPS, SABRIC, PSI, CGRI in Gauteng, South Africa and ECU in Perth, Western Australia, for giving me written permission and support to conduct the case study research.

- Special thanks to Dr David Brooks and his team from ECU for making all the appointments for my interviews in Perth, Western Australia. The hospitality shown to me in Australia was wonderful.

- All participants from the security industry in Gauteng who assisted me with the semi-structured and focus group interviews.

- University of South Africa for affording me the opportunity to develop in knowledge and experience through this research.

- To my dearest wife Chumpa, and children Anusha, Kreesen and Kieron who always supported me in my endeavours.

Preface and overview

Security is both a state of being and a means to that end. As a state of being, security suggests two quite distinct objective and subjective conditions. And as an objective condition, it takes a number of possible forms. Firstly, it is the condition of being without threat: the hypothetical state of absolute security. Secondly, it is defined by the naturalisation of threats: the state of being protected from. Thirdly, it is a form of avoidance or non-exposure to danger ... As a subjective condition, security again suggests both the positive condition of feeling safe and freedom from anxiety or apprehension defined negatively by reference to insecurity.

— Zedner, 2003: 155

This book was written to enlighten security officials about security information management, which includes the collection and analysis of information on security incidents, threats and vulnerabilities and the implementation of security risk control measures. It is hoped that the reader will now have an idea how to collect security information legally and ethically, using different sources, methods and techniques, as well as analyse security information according to the needs of the client and transforming the analysis results into actionable crime information products, strategies and physical protection systems (PPS) be implemented as security risk control measures. It is hoped that the reader will understand the difference between security information management and security risk management as well as other information and intelligence management strategies. The book presents a security information management model (SIMM) to guide security practitioners in their daily activities.

OVERVIEW

Presently, the security industry comprises private and government security service providers. They are divided into different sectors according to the security service function they perform. Each sector has a specific goal and emphasis in respect of security-related functions.

The substantive grounded theory that was developed by the author describes how security information is presently managed in the security industry. The substantive grounded theory also forecasts that if security information is not managed correctly, there will be a continuous recurrence of losses. The substantive grounded theory in this research was developed by obtaining qualitative data through focused semi-structured interviews and focus group interviews. The collected data was manually coded and categorised by the author. It was not difficult to develop a "story line" which started with the collection of security information, continued with its analysis and ended with the implementation of security risk control measures.

Selective coding resulted in the following conclusion: the core category that emerged after coding was the security officials' "management of security information." The core category was developed in the same way as all the other categories and a substantive grounded theory emerged. The theory is that security officers manage security information without a model. This created an opportunity for the author to design and develop a model for security information management. This model was discussed with specific security experts in South Africa. They were strongly in favour of the security information management model (SIMM) to enhance security information management in South Africa. The security information model is briefly explained below.

Security information management is spread out in three phases, namely the collection of security information phase; analysis of security information phase; and the implementation of security risk control measures phase. The Security Information Management Centre (SIMC) handles the collection and analysis of the security information and refers it to top management as an analysis report (result/outcome). Top management handles the analysis report and refers it to the operational manager or the human resources manager for the application of security risk control measures.

Phase 1: Collection of security information

Planning and/or direction

A strategic plan is developed by the Board of Directors and Executive Level Management. The strategic plan among others identifies the security threats affecting the organisation and its assets, as well as an organisational security strategy to address the threats.

Target-centred approach

The organisation should identify its targets, which may include critical assets or information, people, or critical areas and processes.

Collection of security information

Once a shared target has been identified, it is time to prepare a collection plan to focus on the threats and vulnerabilities affecting the shared target. The senior security officer should develop and manage this collection plan in accordance with project management principles. The collection plan should be developed in consultation with the security analyst. The security analyst should be able to provide guidance on the kinds of information to be collected and the key information needs to prepare specific analysis products in terms of the organisational security strategy. Security information about threats, incidents and vulnerabilities should be lawfully collected in a structured manner within the ambit of an organisational policy framework. Standard operating procedures in line with the organisational policy framework should be developed to guide the collection of the different kinds of security information. A collection unit should be established within the Security Information Management Centre (SIMC) to collect security information and to service the analysts in the collection of missing information. The Security Information Management Centre should manage all the collected information and provide rapid response to security information that requires immediate action.

Sharing of security information

There should be a plan for the sharing of information. Funding should be available for training, infrastructure, the development of standards, and the building of trust between law enforcement and the security service providers. Informal information-sharing networks are used when formal systems prove to be too tedious.

Phase 2: Analysis of security information

The security analyst should identify the kinds of security information as well as the key information needs. All the collected security information should be managed by the SIMC who should have the information evaluated/verified and entered into a computerised database. All security information is collated by the analyst or a data capturer using an automated system with the relevant computer software. This includes indexing, sorting, and storing of raw information. A database should be created for storage. Only when similar information is collected and considered together, can the analyst provide meaning to the information. The SIMC manager may task the collection unit to obtain missing information to ensure data integrity of the collected security information. All threat information should be collated on the Threat Assessment field, while vulnerabilities should be collated on the vulnerability assessment (VA) field. The computerised system can also be designed to provide for an Incident Register to record all information on incidents. A computerised database will allow for the use of software to collate and analyse data into actionable information.

An analysis function should be centralised because security information works on the principle of bringing together all relevant bits and pieces of data and information and adding meaning to it. The analysis capability should be situated at the SIMC. The development of an effective analysis capability, really, is the true justification for establishing the SIMC.

Key information needs

The analyst should access the collected security information from the computer to confirm the key information needs and provide an analysis result in line with the organisational security strategy. Analysis of security information entails evaluation and interpretation of the exact nature of the problem and the characteristics of the incidents, threats and vulnerabilities. Important factors to consider include where the incidents are occurring, at what times, who is involved, how and why the problem is occurring, and what solutions have been tried in the past. By determining the underlying causes of the problem through the collection of detailed information, more effective tactical strategies can be developed to address the problem.

Collecting missing information

Once the analyst has determined the key information needs and what information is missing or unavailable and where to find it, new tasking should be given to the collection unit or the responsible person for additional information. This new information will be used to enrich the information on hand, so that an accurate, complete analysis result can be produced.

Evaluation and interpretation

The evaluation phase is the true analysis phase and has three aspects, that is, assessing, integrating and interpreting the information. The reliability of the information source is assessed on specific criteria such as the previous quality of information supplied by the source, the situation, the location, and likely access of the source, at the time, to the information collected. The accuracy of the information provided is assessed as an actual relative measurement in relation to each item of information received. Although the reliability of the source needs to be assessed, the credibility of the information is also important and should not be neglected. The more primary information is used, the higher the importance of testing because of the subjective nature of human sources and the danger of mistaking misinformation and disinformation for fact. The information as well as where it was sourced, should also be tested for credibility and usability. The interpretation of information is the true analysis function. It requires highly skilled and experienced security information analysts. These skills should include a variety of crime analysis tools, threat analysis tools, vulnerability analysis tools and criticality assessment tools. Incident pattern analysis (IPA) will consist of incident patterns of both crime incidents and policy violation incidents.

Analysis result

Once the evaluation and interpretation have been completed and having determined how the analysis results should best be presented to management, the analysis results now need to be packaged. The analysis result should only consist of the answer to the original question and should not include comprehensive reports in which the answer is indiscernible.

Phase 3: Implementation of security risk control measures

Analysis report

Upon receipt of the analysis report, top management may decide on the application thereof. They may use the analysis result to design appropriate security risk control measures that would deter, detect, delay and respond to an intruder or institute a disciplinary enquiry and/or a civil or criminal prosecution.

Objectives

To formulate objectives, the designer must understand the organisational operations and conditions, define the threat, and identify the target. The ultimate objective of a security plan should be to reduce crime, increase detection and prevent losses. Typical objectives will be to prevent sabotage of critical equipment, theft of assets or information from within the facility, and protection of people. The envisaged security risk control measures must be able to accomplish its objectives through deterrence or a combination of detection, delay, and response.

Design

Using the objectives for security risk control measures obtained in the organisational characterisation, threat definition and target identification, the specialist can design specific security risk control measures. The security risk control measure design must be able to detect and detain (arrest) the adversary, prevent the criminal conduct or irregularity of the adversary from occurring and create awareness to prevent losses. In designing a specific physical protection system to avert the threat identified in the analysis report, management must ensure that the new physical protection system will detect the adversary, delay the adversary, and alert the response force to interrupt the adversary. Security risk control measures may be designed to include strategies encompassing crime prevention through environmental design (CPTED). The challenge is for security managers to make themselves aware of current and innovative design strategies. This knowledge should be coupled with the latest information on issues of changes in cultural values, crime, technology, market conditions, and political conditions.

Dissemination

Dissemination can be carried out in several different ways, namely, through briefings and strategy sessions, presenting verbal reports, providing written reports, having face-to-face contact whenever the need arises, and public information systems – written and electronic media.

Implementation

The end user receives the recommended security risk control measure from management for implementation. The security risk control measure may take the form of strategies, physical protection systems (PPS) or actionable information products. There should be open communication between management, analyst and end user.

Feedback

The last aspect after the implementation of the security risk control measure is feedback and reaction. Management and the analyst need to know what works and what does not work. Feedback may be given verbally or in written format.

Monitoring and evaluation

Once the security risk control measures have been implemented, they must be periodically evaluated to determine the effectiveness or lack thereof. There are two main types of evaluations. They are outcomes and process evaluations. An outcome evaluation is to determine if the security risk control measure had the desired effect, such as, "Was crime reduced?" or "Was an intruder disrupted?" Line management should carry out monitoring and evaluation. It has to begin with a review and thorough understanding of the protection objectives the designed security risk control measure must meet. The PPS should be quantitatively and qualitatively monitored and evaluated for vulnerabilities on a continuous basis.

CHAPTER 1

General orientation

OBJECTIVES

- Discuss the historical context relating to security information management
- Discuss what constitutes a traditional approach in the management of security information
- Critique the statement, "Overprotection of a non-essential entity or failure to adequately protect a vital portion of a facility"
- Appraise the need for a model for the management of security information

---

INTRODUCTION

This book is about managing security information on incidents, threats and vulnerabilities. Incident-based information refers to a variety of events, including for instance an accident, anecdote (bird flies into a camera), or violation of law or of company policy. Reference is made to threat information as information on crimes, criminals, victims, commercial or industrial competitors and people with malicious intent to harm an entity. Security measures are emphasised as the source of information on vulnerabilities and risks. This book has been written with the support of security managers, security officials and stakeholders from different sectors of the security industry, both private and in government. By the end of the book the reader will have a good idea of the collection and analysis of security information relevant to incidents, threats, and vulnerabilities as well as the implementation of security risk control measures (physical protection systems (PPS), strategies and/or actionable information products).

The management of security information is one of the key functions of a security service provider, whether in-house or contracted. It contributes to a wide range of objectives at every level of security, from the reduction of crime to increasing detection rates and preventing losses. Whatever security objectives it is directed at, the management of security information will involve the collection and analysis of security information and the implementation of security risk control measures. Questions on how security practitioners should respond and manage information on incidents, threats and vulnerabilities have plagued scholars and practitioners for decades. It is still our constant source of discussion and is perhaps debated more so now than before the aftermath of the 11 September 2001 attacks on the World Trade Centre in New York and the Pentagon in Washington, DC.

In writing this book, the author considered the International Risk Management Standard ISO 31000:2009, crime combatting and risk mitigation models used internationally and in South Africa by law enforcement and the private security industry. Besides studies on security risks and the use of incident data to influence the reduction of crime, there has been very little research on the practice, and the circumstances under which security information may be legally and ethically collected, analysed and used in the design and development of security risk control measures.

Against this background, it becomes clear that there is a need for a practical approach to guide security practitioners in the management of security information on incidents, threats and vulnerabilities.

SECURITY INFORMATION MANAGEMENT IN CONTEXT

In the 21st century, we have a number of actors and providers involved in policing. They include the South African Police Service (SAPS), private security, Metro Police, local authority, statutory institutions and community policing structures that provide a specific policing service. This proliferation has led to the pluralisation of policing in the 21st century (Jones and Newburn, 2006). A professional security service is fast gaining momentum in South Africa. Citizens are looking out for every new physical protection system backed up by the latest technology and/or piece of equipment that can safeguard property and give protection against criminal elements. Changes and developments in the security service environment demands innovation and creativity to enhance traditional models related to private security. For many years, society has relied exclusively on law enforcement authorities to prevent and control crime within private and government organisations. Many feel that they can no longer expect law enforcement to look after their interests. Private and government organisations contract security service providers or provide for their own in-house security service. Security information management is important to address the security risks confronting an organisation.

Risk mitigation has a long history, which started about 2400 years ago in ancient Greece, where the Athenians always assessed risks before making decisions (Bernstein, 1996). During the 1990's Australia and New Zealand led the world in Enterprise Risk Management by developing the AZ/NZS 4360:1999 in 1999 as a Risk Management Model. They revised and re-issued the model in 2004 as AZ/NZS 4360:2004. There was no international standard in place at this stage. Only a small number of competing frameworks were regarded as satisfactory. In 2005, the International Standards Organisation (ISO) started work on ISO 31000 using the

AZ/NZS 4360:2004 as its first draft. On 13 November 2009, ISO 31000 was published and received widespread acclaim (Leitch, 2010). Risk management models to mitigate risks were not used formally until the early 1950s. It is accepted that the modern concept of risk management originated in the United States. Technical developments in the United States confronted the insurance industry with a multiplicity of insurable risks so that insurance was purchased on an "all risk" instead of a "specified peril" basis. The consequence of fluctuating premiums directed the attention of top management to the cost of insurance. This gave rise to the development of risk management actions aimed at containing the cost of insurance. Risk managers were also responsible for finding innovative ways and procedures to reduce losses that resulted in the integration of risk control and risk-financing activities. Risk management developed in South Africa in the 1970s (Valsamakis, Vivian and Du Toit, 1996).

Since its inception, Risk Management has been very popular in South Africa. It was the only risk assessment activity which was widely used to contain the costs of insurance. During the 20th century, very little emphasis was placed on the importance of security information management to reduce crime, increase detection and prevent losses. Security service providers in South Africa manage information on crime incidents, policy violations, threats and vulnerabilities differently. SAPS investigates crime incidents in South Africa. In major business entities such as banks, petroleum and retail companies, crime incident information is also coordinated and managed by security information management companies who provide actionable crime information products to these institutions. SAPS investigates threats, and the threat information is handled internally by individual security service providers. Individual security service providers manage vulnerabilities and incidents relating to policy violations.

Depending on the availability of funds, many security service providers mainly focus on the reinforcement of security measures, when an incident occurs. These additional security measures are mainly implemented to overprotect a non-essential asset. This is due to a lack of understanding: of what needs to be protected; and of the surrounding environment. It is absolutely essential that the asset being protected be fully understood in terms of its constraints, expected performance, operations and the circumstances in which it exists. This can only be made possible through the management of relevant information, which the author describes as "security information." The collection and analysis of security information regarding the constraints, expected performance and operations of assets is vital for the design and development of physical protection systems (PPS), strategies and/ or actionable information products with deterrent value.

THE RATIONALE FOR THIS BOOK

The Constitution of the Republic of South Africa, 1996 provides for Community Police Forums (CPFs) and the National Intelligence Coordinating Committee

(NICOC). Both the community and the police use CPFs to share incident-based information, crime tendencies and patterns. Security managers have a responsibility to become part of CPFs in order to share information on crime incidents and threats (South Africa, 1996). The SAPS shares crime information on incidents and threats with private security service providers on a need-to-know basis (Abrie, 2008). In terms of section 3 of the National Strategic Intelligence Act, No. 39 of 1994, crime intelligence may be provided to the SAPS in support of the SAPS' policing function in terms of section 205 (3) of the Constitution (South Africa, 1994; South Africa, 1996). The Private Security Industry Regulatory Act 56 of 2001 does not provide for the collection and analysis of security information and the utilisation of the analysis results for the design and development of security risk control measures. There is no national or shared database on crime information incidents under the control of PSIRA for use by service providers in the Private Security Industry (South Africa, 2001).

On 22 May 2007, in his speech on the Safety and Security Departmental Budget Vote 2007/08, the then South African Minister for Safety and Security, Charles Nqakula, announced that the private security industry had been drawn into partnership with the SAPS in the fight against crime. He indicated that talks regarding "partnership policing" had been initiated between the police and private security. The Minister stated that, "a partnership between private security and the SAPS would be based on information sharing." He called for the "alignment of private security with SAPS operations." He also stated that, "private security should make a start in enhancing their own information-gathering and sharing capabilities. Collected information should be directly shared with SAPS" (Minister for Safety and Security, 2007).

Minister of Police, Mr Nathi Mthethwa, endorsed the above statement on 15 November 2011 at the 2011 Annual Conference of the South African Security Industry Alliance (SIA). He also stated that an ongoing review and measurement of crime statistics in 2010/2011 indicated a decline in both cash-in-transit heists and the cash loss as a result of these heists. He acknowledged that some of these successes were achieved through the security information that the private security industry contributed (DefenceWeb, 2011).

Both ministers should be applauded for their call for a closer working relationship between SAPS and the private security industry. This is a step in the right direction. Working relationships and trust need to be established among security personnel and between law enforcement and security service providers. This will help promote the sharing of security information (Nemeth, 2010: 89–90).

Constitutionally, SAPS is the custodian of all crime information and crime intelligence. Private security service providers have a legal obligation to refer all crime intelligence on threats to SAPS. Individual security service providers may manage security information relating to incidents, threats, vulnerabilities and policy violations. Specific security information management companies, which operate under the auspices of Business against Crime (BAC) share information with SAPS on a daily basis. They include security information management companies such as the South African Banking Risk Information Centre (SABRIC), Petroleum Security Initiative

(PSI), and Consumer Goods Risk Initiative (CGRI) of the Consumer Goods Council of South Africa (CGCSA) and many others. However, this is limited to crime incident information. Individual private security service providers manage security information on policy violations and vulnerabilities (Maree, 2010).

Security service providers gain some understanding of the state of security of the assets they protect through formal and informal sources of information. These sources include customer contacts, incidents at the workplace and information collected using human and technical means. Information from these sources is not always comprehensive in nature. The information may sometimes be tacitly affected by the source's own perception, knowledge, and other psychological factors. They are often forms of fragmented information that provide an inaccurate picture of the state or status of security. A security service provider can gain a comprehensive understanding of the current state of security and its deficiencies by means of proper security information management. Proper planning is needed to ensure that security information is managed according to organisational standards and objectives (Johnson, 2005). It is important that all the employees, security officials and clients of the organisation get involved in the management of security information, which in general does not seem to be the case in most organisations. In many organisations, the collection of security information is not guided by a strategic plan, organisational security strategy, security plan and a collection plan. These documents are essential to provide direction to the collectors of the security information and to avoid waste of human resources and technology in collecting security information that the client does not need. According to Garcia (2008), these documents will define the threats, vulnerabilities and all reported incidents. The collection of security information should be directed at potential threats, vulnerabilities and incidents related to the threat.

Security information is not always analysed by qualified and experienced security information analysts. Supervisors and security practitioners mainly use the raw information for resource deployment in critical areas, to prevent a recurrence of an incident. According to Garcia (2006: 1), for the sake of accuracy, reliability and validity, qualified experienced analysts should be employed to organise the information into threat assessment, vulnerability assessment (VA) and IPA documents, so that it becomes usable as guiding instruments.

Analysed results should be utilised for addressing specific threats and vulnerabilities according to the organisational security strategy. According to Johnson (2005), collected security information should be analysed timely and used for the implementation of security risk control measures as soon as the threat or vulnerability analysis result is known. The security risk control measures may take the form of physical protection systems (PPS), strategies and actionable crime information products (Fischer, Halibozek and Green, 2008). Many security service providers have been doing informal collection and analysis of security information and the implementation of security risk control measures for many years. However, they still do not have a model similar to the Risk Management Model ISO 31000:2009 to guide them in this regard.

Security information management is a growing issue in all spheres be it industry or government and affects management positions at different authority levels, from the end user to board level. All employees of an organisation should understand the importance of security information management and how they, as employees, are responsible for their actions in the workplace. It is important that security information be managed according to strategy, policy and standard operating procedures.

A security information management culture is about creating awareness on the importance of security information management to reduce crime, increase detection rates and prevent losses (Garcia, 2008: xvii; Reuland, 1997). All employees in an organisation should be made aware of their role in and responsibility for the collection and analysis of security information and the utilisation of security information products. Employees should be encouraged to intensify the collection of security information using open sources of information (Clark, 2010; Newburn, Williamson and Wright, 2008). In an ever-changing environment, organisations must try to create and sustain a healthy security information management culture. A security information management culture focuses on encouraging proper planning and management of all security information issues in the organisation, especially since organisations are dependent on data, raw information, information systems and networks. Security information management must become part of the day-to-day operations of employees. Instilling a strong security culture in an organisation can help to ward off threats, incidents and irregularities. If boards of directors want their organisations to survive, they have to change their culture and keep up with current security information management developments. Cultivating a culture of security information management among stakeholders will ensure the safety of all assets of the organisation. Security awareness programmes will be essential to cultivate a security information management culture (Kritzinger, 2006).

Corporate governance is a responsibility enforced by law in countries such as South Africa and England (King, 1994). Corporate governance must be taken seriously because the accountability for corporate governance ultimately rests with a company/ organisation's board and executive management. If the corporate governance system fails in an organisation, it will be bound to lose its competitive edge and will not be able to ensure its survival. In South Africa, all companies seeking public listings need to show corporate governance of the management of risks in their companies (Shaw, 2002).

There is no section in the King Reports 1, 2 and 3 that covers the management of security information per se. The board and executive management in organisations are still accountable for security information management in their organisations. Security information governance involves the leadership, organisational structure, processes and technologies used for the collection and analysis of security information and the implementation of security risk control measures. The managers at the level of board and executive management can be taken to court if the integrity, availability or confidentiality of information is compromised in any way. It is also essential that corporate governance include information security as a vital part of governing an organisation, and also that the board and executive management levels should encourage effective and responsible use of information among all stakeholders in the organisation (Kritzinger, 2006).

Many security service providers in South Africa have information security policies to ensure ongoing information security. "Information security policies are there to ensure the identification, authentication, authorisation, confidentiality, integrity and non-repudiation of information" (Kritzinger, 2006: 6; 74). Before any organisation can start to secure their information, they should first have security information management policies, plans, and strategies in place as a guideline on what must be managed and how it must be managed. These policies should encourage open door information sharing based on specific conditions (Ratcliffe, 2009). Top management is responsible for the formulation of these policies, plans and strategies. These security information policies/plans/strategies should relate to the collection and analysis of security information and the implementation of security risk control measures. Middle management has to ensure that information is collected, analysed and implemented according to standard operating procedures as outlined in policy/plans and strategies (Smit and Cronje, 2002).

Security information management is a fundamental part of security management. This concept needs proper planning, organising, leadership, coordination and control to be successful. The concept ensures that policy follows strategy. This security framework for the management of security incidents, threats and vulnerabilities should be seen as a concept separate from security risk management, which was introduced to prevent losses so that insurance premiums may be reduced. The primary reason for this study was to provide a framework to regulate the management of security information, to collect and analyse security information and to use the analysis results in the design and development of strategies, PPS, and/or actionable information products. This security information management model (SIMM) should be seen as a concept to reduce crime, increase detection and reduce losses (Nemeth, 2010). Academic disciplines have advanced over centuries through developments and new trends that have changed the face of security operations worldwide. What is important is that we should learn from the lessons that are present in these developments and new trends, so that we can modify and apply those that have the potential to assist us in our daily activities.

Specific policing and security management models used in the last decade, such as problem-oriented policing (POP), Compstat, intelligence-led policing (ILP) and various security risk management models (SRMMs) bear testimony to attempts by law enforcement and the private security industry to reduce crime, increase detection rates and prevent losses. These models used by law enforcement and security practitioners in crime combatting and security risk mitigation serves as the departure point for this book. These models are discussed in chapter 4 in this book.

AIM AND OBJECTIVES OF THE BOOK

The aim of this book is to get uniformity and consistency within the private security industry and to demonstrate the theoretical and practical thinking of security information management. Since the International Standards Organization (ISO) only propagates the ISO 31000:2009 as a generic Risk Management Model, which puts forward principles, a framework and process, that provide for the identification, analysis, evaluation, treatment, monitoring, and communication of risk. Based on the Risk Management Model ISO 31000:2009 and other similar crime combatting and risk mitigation models, this study explored the security information management practices in both private and government organisations, in Gauteng, South Africa and Perth in Western Australia, who use in-house and contracted private security service providers. The reason for bringing in Australia and doing a comparative study between South Africa and Australia is that Australia, together with New Zealand, was one of the countries that led the world in Enterprise Risk Management. Furthermore, Edith Cowan University (ECU) in Perth, offers an educational qualification similar to South Africa on Security Risk Management. The author was convinced that the only way of finding out about developments and new trends in security information management, was to obtain clarity on current security industry practices in South Africa and Australia in terms of serving both the private and government sectors, and to identify the nature and extent of problems experienced in collecting, analysing and implementing security risk control measures.

To provide a book which is scientifically based, the author qualitatively studied security information management practices in the security industry, using the grounded theory design. The grounded theory design was used to explore the security information management practices both in private and government organisations in Gauteng, South Africa and Perth in Western Australia. The assumption was that the collection, analysis and the implementation of security risks control measures is not strategically driven by a model.

ORGANISATION OF THE BOOK

Based on the historical contextualisation and the rationale for this book, the aim and objectives were achieved as outlined below:

Chapter 2: Concepts in security information management

This chapter shows that South Africa, as a developing nation needs to acquaint itself with international standards. The knowledge domain of security information management in South Africa is yet to achieve its professional status to be designated as an academic discipline.

Chapter 3: Security information management in practice

This chapter provides grounded data on the current approach to security information management in both South Africa and Australia. The purpose thereof is to set the context for a model and to make recommendations.

Chapter 4: The need for a theoretical framework for security information management

This chapter discusses crime information, intelligence and SRMMs as well as the need for a theoretical framework for security information management. It is important to remember that the management of security information regarding incidents, threats and vulnerabilities is the golden thread that runs right through this book.

Chapter 5: Security information management model

This chapter identifies present problems in the management of security information and provides recommendations and an exposition of a model that outlines the security information management framework for the collection and analysis of security information on incidents, threats and vulnerabilities and the implementation of security risk control measures.

Chapter 6: Security information management process

This chapter discusses the security information process as outlined in the SIMM. It is now the time for the security industry to play a greater role in the prevention and control of crime and losses than ever before.

Chapter 7: Summary

In this final chapter, attention is given to incident, threat and vulnerability management and its relationship to the management of security information in South Africa.

CHAPTER 2

Concepts in security information management

OBJECTIVES

- **Define** the concept of security information management.

- **Defend** a framework that supports a contextual definition of security information management.

- **Discuss** the concepts: security information collection, analysis, and security risk control measures.

- **Critique** the Private Security Industry Regulatory Act, 56 of 2001.

INTRODUCTION

The discussion and definitions of key concepts in this chapter are important for two reasons: firstly, to provide clarity as far as the use of these concepts are concerned, and, secondly, to provide an early indication of the direction of the discussions in this book. Different definitions and interpretations of important concepts were discovered in the literature and other sources, including official publications and personal interviews. For some concepts, no definitions could be found, hence a "lay person's" interpretation was provided to give meaning to its application. It is important to define and discuss the key concepts, so that readers will have a common understanding of the important concepts. The following important concepts will be explained:

- security

- security service

- security management

- security information management

- security incident

- security threat

- security vulnerability

- security information collection

- security information analysis
- security risk control measures

SECURITY

"Security implies a stable, relatively predictable environment in which an individual or group may pursue its ends without disruption or harm and without fear of such disturbance or injury" (Fischer, Halibozeck, and Green, 2008). According to Smith and Brooks (2013), a traditional definition of security may be the provision of private services in the protection of people, information and assets for individual safety or community wellness. In addition, Post and Kingsbury (1991), consider the security of private and commercial property as the provision of paid services in preventing undesirable, unauthorised, or detrimental loss to an organisations assets. Private security refers to those efforts by individuals and organisations to protect their assets from loss, harm or reduction in value, due to threats. These assets may include people, fixed and immovable property, business rights, information, company image, operational strategies, contracts, agreements and policy (Bosch, 1999).

SECURITY SERVICE

According to section 1 (1) of the Private Security Industry Regulatory Act, 56 of 2001: "Security service" means one or more of the following services or activities:

- protecting or safeguarding a person or property in any manner;
- providing a reactive response service in connection with the safeguarding of a person or property in any manner;
- giving advice on the protection or safeguarding of a person or property or the use of security equipment;
- providing a service aimed at ensuring order and safety on premises used for sporting, recreational, entertainment or similar purposes;
- manufacturing, importing, distributing or advertising of monitoring devices contemplated in section 1 of the Interception and Monitoring Prohibition Act 127 of 1992;
- providing services related to the functions of an investigator;
- providing security training or instruction to a security service provider or prospective service provider;
- monitoring signals or transmissions from electronic security equipment;
- installing, servicing or repairing security equipment;

- **perform**ing the functions of a locksmith; and
- **manag**ing, controlling or supervising the rendering of any of the above **servic**es (South Africa, 1992; South Africa, 2001).

"**Privat**e security" refers to those efforts by individuals and organisations to protect their **assets** from loss, harm or reduction in value, due to threats. These assets may **include** people, fixed and immovable property, business rights, information, company **image**, operational strategies, contracts, agreements and policy (Bosch, 1999).

In terms of section 1 (1) of the Private Security Industry Regulatory Act, No. 56 of **2001**, "a security officer is defined as any natural person who is employed by another **person**, including an organ or department of the State and who receives or is entitled **to receive** from such other person any remuneration, reward, fee or benefit, for **rendering** one or more security services" (South Africa, 2001).

SECURITY MANAGEMENT

"**Management** may be defined as the process of planning, organising, leading and **controlling** the resources of an organisation to achieve the stated organisational goals **as productively** as possible" (Smit and Cronje, 2002: 9). In any organisation effective **security** management can only be achieved through proper inputs and outputs. These **include** various security enablers such as strategic and tactical direction and alignment, **leadership**, governance, accountability, ethics, culture, sustainability and resilience. **Finally**, outputs need to be clearly articulated in as much as what should be achieved **from** security management. These outputs include the protection of people, **information**, and assets, as well as stakeholder assurance, maintained capability, legal **and social** compliance, and confidence in the organisation so that learning is achieved. **To gain** acceptance from the executive decision-makers, security managers must **understand** the organisation's culture, clearly define the security role, and know when **and when** not to raise alarm bells. In today's ever-changing threat environment, there **is a need** for more dynamic and proactive security management. Security management **mitigates** negative risks; puts in place response, control, and recovery plans should **prevention** measures fail; and does not overlook or jeopardise potential business **opportunities**. All of these factors and more can be brought together through **competent** security management (Smith and Brooks, 2013).

MANAGEMENT OF SECURITY INFORMATION

Security information management includes the process of planning, organising, leading and controlling the collection, analysis and dissemination of the analysis results for use in the implementation of security risk control measures and obtaining feedback on the utilisation thereof. According to Peterson (1994), Security Information Management is the act of collecting information that will enable an analyst to make a recommendation on the implementation of PPS, strategies and/or actionable information products to mitigate security risks.

SECURITY INCIDENT

Security incident information refers to information regarding any event or occurrence resulting from a threat or policy violation (Allen, 1992).

SECURITY THREAT

An individual or group with the motivation and capability for crime, terrorism, foreign intelligence, commercial or industrial competition and malice or other malevolent acts that would result in loss of assets at a facility is a threat (Garcia, 2001). A threat refers to anything that has the potential to prevent and hinder the achievement of objectives or disrupt the processes that support them (Talbot and Jakeman, 2008).

SECURITY VULNERABILITY

Security vulnerability refers to an exploitable capability or an exploitable security weakness or deficiency at a facility of security interest. Exploitable capabilities or weaknesses are those inherent in the design (or layout) of the facility and its protection or those existing because of the failure to meet (maintain) prescribed security standards when evaluated against requirements for defined threats. If an adversary had detected and exploited the vulnerability, then it would reasonably be expected to result in a successful attack causing damage to the facility (Garcia, 2001).

SECURITY INFORMATION COLLECTION

Security information collection is the act of gathering information that will be used to produce a threat assessment, vulnerability assessment (VA), incident pattern analysis (IPA) and an analysis result for use by security practitioners in the design and development of strategies, PPS, and/or actionable information products (Peterson, 1994). Information can be obtained from what a person experiences through his/her five senses. Information can also be obtained from rumours and so-called stories. It includes any raw information or data that has been collected but not analysed. The challenge is to analyse the information or data to determine what is usable and what is unusable (Van Rooyen, 2008).

The term "security information" relates to information on incidents, threats and vulnerabilities, which have the potential to adversely affect an organisation's assets (Fischer et al., 2008; Blyth and Kovacich, 2006). Threat information includes information on criminals, terrorists, foreign intelligence services, commercial or industrial competitors and people with malicious intent to harm the organisation (Garcia, 2001; Talbot and Jakeman, 2008). Information on vulnerabilities is emphasised in specific security measures, projected through people assets, information assets, physical assets/information and communication technology (Talbot and Jakeman, 2008).

SECURITY INFORMATION ANALYSIS

Security information analysis is the reviewing of data and the comparison of it to other data to determine its meaning or relation to other data. This includes different forms of analyses such as evaluation, collation, incident pattern analysis (IPA), vulnerability assessment (VA), threat assessment, and criticality assessment (Peterson, 1994). Evaluation (verification) of security information is the assessment of the reliability of the source and the quality of the information (Jordaan, 2003a). Information collation is the sorting, indexing and storing of information into a format from which it can be retrieved and analysed (Lyman, 1988). The different analysis concepts of importance to the reader are as follows:

IPA in the security industry will consist of incident patterns of both crime incidents and policy violation incidents. Ekblom (1988) describes the IPA process as transforming the original information, which in many instances is typically in the form of an incident report, into a number of variables (type of incident, time and location, method used), and to develop within each variable a number of mutually exclusive categories (for the type of incident and focusing on the incident). According to Gottlieb, Arenberg and Singh (1994), IPA contains information relative to continuing occurrence of particular incidents. This IPA acquaints officers with the types of incidents taking place; lists the days, times and locations of their occurrence; and provides officers with any known suspects, suspect vehicles, modus operandi and/or property loss information. Information concerning the preferred target of attack (victim and/or property) should also be included, as should results of past analyses or predictions as to when and where suspects may strike again.

Vulnerability analysis is a method of identifying the weak points of a facility. It is a systematic evaluation process in which qualitative and/or quantitative techniques are applied to detect vulnerabilities and to arrive at an effectiveness level for a security system to protect specific targets from specific adversaries and their acts (Garcia, 2001). A VA involves a process or outputs associated with reviewing assets and or security systems to identify weaknesses. Usually conducted from a baseline on how they could fail or be successfully attacked (Talbot and Jakeman, 2008).

Threat analysis is a process in which information about a threat or potential threat is subjected to systematic and thorough examination in order to identify significant facts and derive conclusions (Garcia, 2001). Threat assessment is a judgment, based on available intelligence, law enforcement and open source information, of the actual or potential threat to one or more assets (Garcia, 2001). According to Le Roux (2004), threat assessment is the identification of potentially undesirable events that could result in loss or harm.

Criticality assessment attempts to prioritise organisational infrastructure, assets or elements by the relative importance or dependence on that element. In practice, this is often related to the magnitude of downstream impacts created by the element's destruction or disablement. Criticality assessment may be based on the magnitude of potential casualties, long-term effects on organisational objectives and economic or socio-political impacts (Talbot and Jakeman, 2008).

"The term has been defined as the impact of a loss as measured in rands." In addition to the cost of the lost item, it also includes replacement costs, temporary replacement, downtime, discounted cash, insurance rate changes and the loss of marketplace advantage (Fischer et al., 2008: 157–158).

SECURITY RISK CONTROL MEASURES

According to Le Roux (2004), security risk is defined as the chance or likelihood of an undesirable event occurring and causing harm or loss. The key element of risk here is uncertainty, without which there is no risk. The analysis of the collected security information will identify specific risks that will need security measures. These risks will require the implementation of specific security risk control measures. The security risk control measures may take the form of PPS, strategies and actionable crime information products (Fischer et al., 2008).

According to Rogers (2008), security risk control measures refer to all the security measures that must be implemented for deterrence, deflection, detection, delay, reaction, identification, rectifying identified security weaknesses, detention of perpetrators and the recovery of losses from insurance.

Physical protection systems (PPS) refer to measures implemented for the protection of assets or facilities against criminals, terrorists, foreign intelligence services, commercial or industrial competitors, malicious people or other malevolent attacks (Garcia, 2001). Strategies refer to overall methods planned by the adversary to achieve its objectives (Garcia, 2001). Strategic actionable information products are generally research oriented, involving inferential and multivariate statistics; they include crime trend forecasts, resource allocation and situational analysis. Tactical actionable information products involve pattern detection, linkage analysis for suspect-crime correlations, target profiling and offender movement patterns (Goldsmith, McGuire, Mollenkopf and Ross, 2000).

Dissemination is the release of recommendations for the implementation of PPS/ strategies and/or actionable information products to a client under certain conditions and protocols (Peterson, 1994). Feedback refers to informing the analyst of the outcome of the implementation of specific PPS/ strategies and/ or actionable information products (Reuland, 1997).

CONCLUSION

Since the concept of "security" means different things to different people, the ability to define and understand the concept of security is open to debate. The diverse and multidimensional nature of this broad concept can be easily understood, if it can be contextually defined. The distinction while being diverse has a common thread to security science. As an emerging academic discipline, it is considered in this book as an objective, subjective and symbolic perspective, which allows different concepts, theories and ideas to be considered collectively. The different concepts discussed in this chapter can be integrated and expanded into a standardised model to regulate the management of security information.

Security information management in practice

OBJECTIVES

- Critically discuss the conceptualised assumptions generated through the grounded data.

- Defend the functioning of Security Information Management Companies.

- Discuss the security information management model used in Western Australia.

- Compare the security industry in Gauteng, South Africa with that of Perth in Western Australia.

INTRODUCTION

This chapter focuses on security information management practices used by security service providers in the Gauteng province of South Africa and in Perth, Western Australia. Research on the management of security information was conducted in Gauteng, South Africa and in Perth, Western Australia using the grounded theory design. This strategy was used to accurately determine how security information is managed in private and government organisations in both countries. The researcher held a social constructivist worldview that officials understand the world in which they live and work better than anyone not specifically working in their environment. Therefore, the researcher relied as much as possible on the one-on-one interviews and focus group interviews. Simultaneously, there was a need to understand the responses provided by the participants and to interpret their meaning, so that a theory or pattern of meaning could be generated and inductively developed from the grounded data. Using one-on-one interviews and focus group discussions, the author was directly involved with the participants in the study. Data was collected in the form of written and spoken language using an interview schedule and an interview guide for the focus group interviews. The researcher collected qualitative data from selected security managers, security officials and other stakeholders relating to their own practical experiences on security information management. In so doing, the researcher gained an understanding of the worldview of security practitioners based on their knowledge and experience.

17

The grounded theory design was used to analyse the data so that a grounded theory could be inductively constructed to contribute to the scientific body of knowledge for this specific discipline. The researcher found the grounded theory design to be a systematic way of developing and integrating this scientific knowledge and information. The open, axial and selective coding procedures were used to generate the grounded theory. This involved generating themes and categories of information, selecting subcategories and positioning it with specific categories and themes within a theoretical model. It then involved explicating a story from the interconnection of these themes and categories and establishing a core category. The grounded theory was generated from the themes, categories and story line. A selective coding process was used for the selection of a core category. The process unfolded through a systematic relation to other categories, validating those relationships and filling in categories that needed further refinement and development. The selective coding process resulted in the following conclusion: the core category that emerged after coding was the security officials' "management of security information." The grounded theory is that security officials do not manage security information by using a standardised model. Given the nature of security information management practices in South Africa and Perth in Western Australia, the grounded data was used to generate the assumptions discussed below.

Security officials did not know the strategic objectives of the organisation being protected or what the needs of the client were; as a result, money, human resources and technology were wasted on collecting security information that is not relevant to the organisation. This waste of resources is not good for an organisation whose reason for existence is profit-making or service delivery. The assumption is that a strategy or plan is not strategically driving the collection of security information

There was no mention that qualified analysts were compiling an incident pattern analysis, threat assessment and a VA for use by security service providers. It would seem as though the focus was on looking at daily security incidents and making a decision to reinforce security measures where necessary, depending on the availability of funds. Security supervisors made a random decision with little or no input from management. There was no mention of an analysis capacity to address information on security incidents, specific threats and vulnerabilities. Some bigger security service providers do prepare crime reports on trends, profiles on suspicious suspects, hot spot areas and crime assessments; however, these are not done by specialist analysts, but by ex-police officials or administration officials. The assumption is that there is no specific analysis capacity operating under qualified analysts employed to do analysis on security incidents, threats, and vulnerabilities.

The implementation of security risk control measures is not considered in conjunction with the organisation's security plan. Security information is collected randomly (without any structure, benchmarks or integration) without knowing the client's specific security needs. A decision to implement or not to implement the security risk control measure is only taken after money, human resources and technology had been invested in the collection and analysis of the security information (analysis done by established private security service providers in exceptional circumstances). Management only decides during the implementation phase not to implement the security risk control measures due to the costs involved. In most cases, the implementation of the security risk control measures is shelved. Much of the security risk control measures implemented are not qualitatively assessed by evaluating its deterrence, detection, delay and response capabilities (and impact after application). The assumption is that objectives such as the reduction of crime, increase in detection rates and the prevention of losses are not considered in the implementation of security risk control measures.

SOUTH AFRICA

Since the late seventies private security development in South Africa was supported by government. Government encouraged the development of the private security industry to fill the vacuum left by the police in the safeguarding of strategic installations. The National Key Points Act, No. 102 of 1980, granted greater powers to the private security guards tasked with guarding and protecting identified strategic installations. The Act granted full powers of arrest, search and seizure to security officers in pursuance of such task (Irish, 1999).

Over the years, the private security industry in South Africa has undergone incredible change. Not only has it seen a growth in the numbers of personnel but also a proliferation and expansion of different sectors in terms of specialisation. In addition, it has also seen a number of changes to its regulatory legislation and controlling framework. All these factors have influenced the focus, profitability and future expansion of the industry. With reference to the regulation, there has over the years been a long process of legislative amendments and regulatory changes aimed at better controlling and monitoring the private security industry in South Africa, specifically in terms of registration, compliance and training standards. Starting with the South African Security Officer's Act, No. 92 of 1987 and the introduction of the Private Security Industry Regulation Act, No. 56 of 2001, a strong regulatory framework for controlling and managing the South African private security industry was established. The Private Security Industry Regulation Act, No. 56 of 2001, essentially set up the Private Security Industry Regulatory Authority (PSIRA) (replacing the Security Officers' Board), as well as obliging every security company inclusive of in-house security to register as a "security service provider" and to have its personnel registered as well. The Act incorporated provisions for a new Code of Conduct and the Improper Conduct Regulations. Furthermore, it established an inspectorate with increased powers of inspection of all registered security service providers with powers of prosecution and reporting of charges of misconduct (Minnaar, 2007).

Private security has grown steadily in recent years, since then identifying market opportunities in government departments and expanding its influence to the realm of community and neighbourhood policing and community safety networks in South Africa (Minnaar, 2005). As of 22 October 2010, 7 459 security companies were registered with PSIRA in the Republic of South Africa. These companies employed 387 273 security officers to work in the Republic of South Africa. As of 4 October 2011, PSIRA had 411 109 registered security officers and 8 828 security companies registered on the PSIRA database (Private Security Regulatory Authority (PSIRA), 2012). In 2014, there were 446 000 registered security officers and 10 000 security companies registered on the PSIRA database (Gumedze, 2015).

The involvement of former intelligence and police personnel has had a marked impact on the security information management skills of private security companies in South Africa (Irish, 1999). This has also helped build a good working relationship between the private security officials and the SAPS. Information is an extremely valuable tool for use by security officials, investigators and police officers for the reduction of crime, to improve detection rates and prevent losses. It is a key element in the sequence of events aimed at conceiving, implementing and evaluating measures to mitigate security risks (Ekblom, 1988). It has proven to be an integral part of the skills package of specialists and experts, whose job it is to prevent and investigate crime and losses successfully. It helps them in reducing crime, making arrests, solving crimes and preventing losses. It is useful for security officials, police officers and investigators to know if a specific crime is on the increase, in which geographic part is it occurring, who is most likely to be committing the crime and where the offender(s) can be found (Lyman, 1988). Conducting analysis on security information makes it possible to devise security risk control measures appropriate to the local crime problem and its physical and social context. The implementation of these measures will require a great deal of commitment, coordination and perseverance. The form of evaluation of the preventative measures will depend on the broader context of a preventative initiative. Evaluation enables managers and practitioners to decide whether the initiative in question has had a sufficient impact on crime to be worth continuing, amending or extending (Ekblom, 1988).

Government departments

Government departments in South Africa have in-house security structures established within departments. These security officials are also registered with PSIRA. They possess civilian powers in terms of the Criminal Procedure Act 51 of 1977. Some in-house security officers employed by specific government departments are empowered by national legislation relevant to the specific government department to carry out their responsibilities. Depending on the business case of the government department, they work with security information on incidents, threats and vulnerabilities. Crime incident information is reported to the SAPS for investigation. All threat information is also reported to SAPS. Government departments address vulnerabilities by applying security risk control measures to mitigate risks. Internal investigators from the human resources section investigate incidents related to policy violations. According to those interviewed for this study, the collection and analysis of security information and the implementation of security risk control measures are not regulated in their departments. None of the service providers who were interviewed made any policy frameworks available. The internet search engines could not provide any such policy frameworks.

Security information is mainly collected by conducting security assessments. Voluntary information is also received from third parties. "Hotline" information is collected by providing toll-free telephone numbers to the public. Some of the methods used to collect security information include surveillance, research (external sources), internal audit (internal sources), forensics and interviews. In some instances, undercover operations are implemented together with the SAPS. The SAPS usually leads this activity. The collected information is entered manually in specific registers (occurrence book, case registers). Security officers in government departments mainly direct their efforts to information collection pertaining to vulnerabilities and incidents related to crime and policy violations. The collection of this type of security information helps them understand the threats facing the department. All criminal matters are referred to the police and workplace investigators investigate incidents of policy violations. Much of the information is incomplete. In most instances, information is received late. Information obtained through direct interviews is always valid and reliable.

In most cases, the collected information is analysed by management and a decision is made on security risk control measures. Very seldom do departments use analysts to evaluate, collate and analyse the information. In some instances, ordinary clerks are used as analysts to determine trends and patterns pertaining to crime. They use computer software to collate and analyse the information. The computer software produces crime pattern analysis products. Vulnerabilities are given attention according to the threat they pose. Management considers the likelihood and consequences of the threat at their meetings. Under normal circumstances, no formal analysis is done on threats and vulnerabilities. Management makes decisions based on the security information placed before them. If the situation warrants it, security risk control measures are implemented based on affordability. There was no indication that probability, impact and cost benefit analyses had been done in this regard. In many instances, there was a dire shortage of personnel, computers and the correct software to collate and analyse the information. If additional information is required, risk managers, security officers or investigators are used to collect this information. Information is classified and handled in terms of the Minimum Information Security Standards (MISS) document[1] (South African Government official, 2010a, 2010b; South African Academic, 2011).

---

1. The Minimum Information Security Standards (MISS) document was approved by the South African Cabinet in 1996, for implementation in all government departments in South Africa.

South African Police Service

Legislative frameworks are provided to regulate the collection of crime intelligence in the country. The South African Police Service (SAPS) has a General as its National Commissioner, Lieutenant-Generals as Provincial Commissioners, Major-Generals are Cluster Commanders and Brigadiers and lower ranks are positioned at police station level. SAPS personnel are provided with guidelines and directives on the management of crime information and intelligence. In terms of security information management SAPS manages information on crime incidents, crime intelligence and threats. They do not manage information on private security vulnerabilities (Reddy, 2010).

SAPS Crime Information Officers (CIOs) at police station level capture all crime incident information reported by victims and complainants on an automated Crime Administration System (CAS). Supervisors validate the information and data capturers enter it into automated systems. This information flow starts from police station level and moves upwards through the automated system to the provincial office and up to the national office. The information is protected through classification in terms of the Minimum Information Security Standards (MISS) policy document. Anyone with valid access to the information can access it. If the person is not allowed to access the information, the CAS will deny access (De Kock, 2011; South African Police Officer, 2011).

The Crime Information Analysis Centre (CIAC) uses the business intelligence system (BIS) to analyse crime information at police station level. Crime Information Officers (CIOs) at police station level are involved in fieldwork to gather crime information through interviews and visiting crime scenes. The collection of this additional crime information is primarily used for addressing the what, why, where, who and how aspects of crime. The new information is used to add value to the existing information on the BIS to generate actionable crime information products for operationalisation at police station level. Some of the actionable crime information products generated by the Crime Information Analysis Centres (CIACs) include crime statistical analysis, crime pattern analysis (CPA), geographic crime analysis, linkage analysis, case docket analysis and profiling. The integration of all the information from these actionable crime information products helps to generate a Crime Threat Assessment (CTA) document at police station level. At police station level, some of the relevant crime information is shared at Community Policing Forums (CPFs) (De Kock, 2011; South African Police Officer, 2011).

This CTA of the police station is integrated at cluster level with the CTAs of the cluster police stations. Hence, a cluster CTA is generated. Linkage analysis is done on the information from the cluster stations. The linkage analysis product is provided to the Crime Intelligence Commanders at cluster level. The information is enriched to produce crime intelligence. The crime intelligence is used to effectively, efficiently, proactively and reactively conduct intelligence-led policing in the cluster (De Kock, 2011; South African Police Officer, 2011).

At provincial level, the cluster information is integrated into a CTA document for intelligence-led operations. Security service providers from both private security and government enrich this intelligence. The Provincial Office has a structured "War Room," which is used to obtain information from these and other stakeholders in the fight against crime. Crime intelligence is not shared with other stakeholders, unless authorised by the Provincial Commissioner (De Kock, 2011; South African Police Officer, 2011).

The information provided by the Provincial CTA is considered at national level to address organised crime using unconventional methods such as undercover operations and specific surveillance methods (De Kock, 2011; South African Police Officer, 2011). At all levels, different methods are used to collect information. Some of the methods include physical surveillance, electronic surveillance, forensics, interviews, research, audits and undercover investigations. Crime Combating Forum (CCF) meetings are held daily at station, provincial and national levels with all stakeholders including private security and other government departments, so that the application of information and intelligence can be monitored and evaluated through crime statistics, arrests and recovery of exhibits. All threat information received from other stakeholders such as private security and government departments are integrated into the CTA at the different operational management levels (De Kock, 2011; Reddy, 2010; South African Police Officer, 2011).

South African private security service providers

Security service providers in Gauteng handle security information on a daily basis. They collect security information on incidents, threats and vulnerabilities. The security information on incidents comprises mainly crime incidents and to a lesser extent policy violations. All the security service providers involved in the research, collect security information. In most instances, information is collected during security assessments by investigators involved in workplace investigations. Some of the methods used to collect security information include surveillance, research (external sources), internal audit (internal sources), forensics, interviews and undercover investigations. Only under exceptional circumstances is undercover investigation conducted in consultation with the SAPS. The research showed that more security information is collected from internal sources compared to external sources. Most of the internal source information consists mainly of reactive information on crime incidents and irregularities that have already taken place at the organisation. This is followed by internal information collected on vulnerabilities using surveillance techniques and security assessments. Much of the external information consists of threats received through hotline reports (toll free) and informer networks. External information on threats mainly originates from other security service providers, organisations, forums and security networks (Conradie, 2010; South African Security Service Provider, 2010a–n).

The majority of the security service providers do not have specific security persons assigned to the collection of security information. Only a few larger organisations/companies have collection units, security risk managers and/or investigators assigned to the collection of security information. This is mainly because of the cost involved in establishing such a capacity. In most cases, the security information is recorded in occurrence books and archived. Security assessments are done at specific intervals. Many security service providers outsource security assessment functions to Risk Management Companies. They are carried out to a lesser extent by in-house security managers due to a lack of knowledge and skills in this regard (Conradie, 2010; South African Security Service Provider, 2010a–n).

All day-to-day, incident-based information is directed to a supervisor and manually recorded in an occurrence book or other similar types of registers. In some instances, they are entered into automated systems for acknowledgement by top management. This is seldom done. Criminal incidents are reported to the SAPS, who registers a case docket for investigation. Criminal incidents relevant to specific business entities are also reported to specific information management companies. The (SAPS) is also informed of all security information on threats, so that responsible intelligence structures in terms of the National Strategic Intelligence Act, No. 39 of 1994 can be activated. The security service provider also initiates strategies in consultation with the police. Security information pertaining to incidents on policy violations are handled by workplace investigators or the human resource section of the company (Conradie, 2010; South Africa 1994; South African Security Service Provider, 2010a–n).

The day-to-day security information received by management is discussed at management meetings and decisions are taken to manage the risk. They inform either the police, human resources section or investigators of the incident or threat. Information on vulnerabilities is handled according to the threat it poses. In many instances, supervisors analyse the information for operationalisation. Only large security service providers have in-house general analysts or specialist analysts. In the majority of cases if additional information is required, security managers, risk managers or investigators are tasked to obtain additional information (Conradie, 2010; South African Security Service Provider, 2010a–n).

When security assessment reports are received from risk management companies, management makes a decision on the implementation of security risk control measures. These decisions are based on the financial position of the companies and the assets being protected. In residential and business complexes, many clients are reluctant to pay an increased premium to implement specific security risk control measures as recommended by the security assessment reports. Consequently, much of the needed security risk control measures are not implemented or are shelved for consideration in the new financial year (Conradie, 2010; South African Security Service Provider, 2010a–n). Many of the security service providers use security information to identify crime trends and patterns and investigative leads. The application of the security information is evaluated by comparing criminal incidents to previous periods (Conradie, 2010; South African Security Service Provider, 2010a–n).

Security Information Management Companies

In recent years specific security information management companies have proven to be successful within specific sectors of the Security Industry. Case studies were conducted with three of these security information management companies to identify their practices.

South African Banking Risk Information Centre

South African Banking Risk Information Centre (SABRIC) is a section 21 security risk information management company established in 2002. It manages and collates crime incident information collected by its clients; analyses the crime incident information and recommends strategies and/or provides actionable crime information products aimed at mitigating organised bank-related crimes. SABRIC adopted a centralised approach to information management, crime analysis and the application of recommended strategies and/ or actionable crime information products. A chief executive officer (CEO), who is supported by a business support office, commercial crime office and violent crime office manages SABRIC. Clients (mainly banks/ financial services organisations) of this company mandated the CEO to do information management and crime analysis and then recommend strategies and/ or provide actionable crime information products to clients, partners and stakeholders. The clients contribute financially, partners mutually benefit and the stakeholders have a stake in the company. The strategic objectives of the company include:

- developing a credible and actionable crime information repository;
- providing leadership that delivers quality services/products and effective strategies to tackle bank-related organised crime;
- coordinating a range of activities to reduce bank-related crime;
- optimising inter-bank cooperation;
- optimising beneficial public private partnerships by interfacing with a range of external organisations, most notably, government departments, law enforcement agencies, regulators and industry associations, both domestically and internationally;
- creating awareness among bank customers and the general public of bank-related crime and ways to prevent it; and
- contributing to the general safety and security of the banking environment (SABRIC, 2010).

South African Banking Risk Information Centre specialises in information management and crime analysis and recommends strategies and/or provides actionable crime information products to its clients, partners and stakeholders. The SABRIC also acts as a source of information to its clients, partners and stakeholders. Daily crime incident information is provided to SABRIC by its clients, partners and stakeholders using their own collection methods and collection means (source techniques). It has standard operating procedures (SOPs) for crime information management, crime analysis and the utilisation of crime information strategies/information products (SABRIC, 2010).

Crime information management

SABRIC's information management strategy is to develop a credible crime information repository with integrity to recommend operational strategies and/ or provide actionable crime information products to clients/partners and stakeholders. Strategies stem from the information in the repository. It is therefore important that the information in the repository is credible. The purpose is thus to develop a credible crime information repository. Collected incident information is not parked on the system and forgotten. Evaluation/Verification of the quality of the information is very important, as it is key to the repository. The consequence management office evaluates/verifies all information on crime incidents received from sources, through follow-up, before the information becomes actionable through analysis. Written information products delivered from this repository such as, updated reports on crime related to Automated Teller Machines (ATMs) is what is termed as an actionable crime information product (SABRIC, 2010).

Standard operating procedures agreed upon by clients, partners and stakeholders are used to ensure credibility and integrity to the crime information provided by clients, partners and stakeholders. Internal sources of information also include the CEO, business support office, and the commercial crime office. A company relies primarily on its clients (banks, cash-in-transit companies, and so on) and its partners (South African Police Service, Metro Police, Business Against Crime). Stakeholders (for instance the Consumer Goods Risk Initiative, Petroleum Security Initiative, and Telkom, among others) and the mass media, would serve as external sources. It does, however use open source techniques to enrich its crime information. The commercial crime office may source information from the violent crime office and vice versa. Consequence management and the information office operate interdependently. If there is an incident, it is given via the information office to the consequence management office to obtain more detail or to enrich the available information (SABRIC, 2010).

There are two types of risks, one is the organised bank-related crime risk, which SABRIC deals with and the other types of security risks are dealt with by the banks themselves. SABRIC cannot manage these risks because of the following factors:

- every individual bank should be looking at what affects them most;
- banks' security models differ;
- they have different service providers from a security point of view; and
- the priorities differ from one bank to another (SABRIC, 2010).

Banks, however, should also have their own analysis capabilities to attend to day-to-day security risks affecting them operationally. Presently, some of them are outsourced to private security contractors who deal predominantly with day-to-day incidents. SABRIC provides a picture of what is happening in the banking industry in general (SABRIC, 2010).

According to the interviewees, they face challenges rather than problems. Some of the challenges include impediments to the constant flow of information from the source to the consequence management office, which is sometimes also not provided according to the criteria set down in the standard operating procedures, for instance, timeliness of the information. The cycle of new staff and restructuring within the partner structure poses a challenge, because they need to be trained to be knowledgeable to meet their challenges. Where technology is concerned, not all their partners and stakeholders have access to computers and not everyone has computer knowledge. Partners do not have cellphones to send (short message system) SMSs, but can receive SMSs and some do not have emails so they use faxes. Some partners operate in outlying areas and cannot be reached due to poor communication infrastructure. Some the clients cannot receive comprehensive reports because of restrictions on their systems. Many clients/ partners/ stakeholders do not have appropriate software programmes and compatibility complicates matters (SABRIC, 2010).

Provinces are visited and particular client representatives including partners are made aware of the company model. Most of the information management challenges are addressed internally and externally through workshops and awareness programmes (SABRIC, 2010).

Crime information analysis

SABRIC has its own analysis infrastructure with in-house analysts. It also outsources specialised analysis functions based on specific needs. The company's analysis strategy is to use all available information from its repository to formulate strategies/ actionable crime information products to mitigate crime, using different computer software programs and human skills. Analysis is done using computer and manual skills. The company recruits highly competent analysts to perform the analysis function. The company starts with initial analysis by collating the data. Information from clients, partners and stakeholders are used in the analysis process. The verification, detail and integrity of the information are very important elements for analysis. Verification of information is done by testing the information against different sources. If the information is not detailed, the missing detail is obtained from the sources. Sources ensure that the information is timely. Information is also enriched by the sources according to standard operating procedures (SOPs). The SOP serves as a memorandum of understanding (MOU), which outlines the procedures that clients, partners, stakeholders and the company must follow. It determines the needs of the clients, partners or stakeholders. These standard operating procedures are contractual by nature. Analysts employed by the company perform a dual function. One such

27

function is to do crime information analyses and the other is to be business minded in the mining of information (SABRIC, 2010).

The security risk information pertaining to organised bank-related crimes is collated, verified, enriched, interpreted and produced as strategies/actionable crime products by the consequence management office for use by clients, partners and stakeholders. Both the consequence management and information offices are sources for one another. They work together. Consequence management serves as a collection unit for information management. If a missing link is identified in the collated information or any additional information is requested, it is passed onto consequence management to do a follow up. The company cannot work with outdated information, it is therefore important that sources provide information on time. It keeps abreast with developments and monitors new methods criminals use in committing crimes. This may also require entering into new partnerships to combat specific types of crimes, for instance, identity thefts, scams, phishing, etc. The consequence managers do linkage analysis, for example using modus operandi and photos received from the bank, etc. They support and assist the investigators and the police to link suspects and crimes with similar modus operandi between cases and suspects (SABRIC, 2010).

The analysts work with modus operandi data, geographic concentrated patterns and statistical information of crime risk factors, data from victims (clients) and explanations of crime. Analysts identify crime patterns, research theoretical explanations and formulate strategies/products for use by the intended users. They also keep abreast with developments in the political, economic, social, technological and international environments to add value to the strategies/actionable products. There is an integrated process all the way. Information is integrated for tactical and strategic purposes. Analysts liaise and verify the repository information with the bank officials or SAPS. Not anybody can amend things on the database. A process needs to be followed if something needs to be amended. Clients, partners and stakeholders do not have access to the database. They have their own databases, which feed into their organisational/company database. They do not have open access to the information. No exchange of information takes place from one database to another due to the agreed upon integrity and credibility of the company database (SABRIC, 2010).

Challenges in analysis are verification (verify information with different sources); detail (not all information is reported in full); integrity (checking on data integrity); and criteria (standards to be followed to collect information). The providers who provide SABRIC with daily crime incident information do not always follow the standard operating procedures (SABRIC, 2010).

Implementation of strategies and actionable crime information products

The company has a policy relating to the implementation of strategies and actionable crime information products. It produces a host of actionable crime information products namely, assessments, briefings, linkage analysis, statistical analysis, association analysis, crime analysis and written reports. Strategies and products are disseminated through briefings, meetings, handouts, reports, e-mails, compact discs, etc. Informational needs of clients, partners and stakeholders are identified in the SOP guideline. Continuous assessment is done on the client's needs in the different environments. Managers hold meetings with clients, partners and stakeholders to determine the needs of the intended users. Clients also request additional information regarding a product (ad hoc request) and this assists with informal feedback. Impact studies are done to determine if all the information received is used accordingly and whether predictions have been realised. Formal meetings, one-on-one interviews, quarterly client surveys and annual partner surveys are used to do follow-ups on disseminated strategies/actionable information products (SABRIC, 2010).

Not just any person can add information to the database or access the database. Staff members are limited in the type of information they can add or access. Two levels of classification are used namely, confidential and restricted. Staff members do not have problems to access the database; they need to have security clearance. Classified access to the database gives credibility to the data in the database (SABRIC, 2010).

The South African Police Service has acknowledged that SABRIC has a big role to play in supporting its operations. Some of the challenges in the application of services, strategies and products is the leakage of information and not getting timely feedback from the intended users. These challenges are addressed internally and externally through workshops and awareness programmes. (SABRIC, 2010).

Consumer Goods Risk Initiative

The Consumer Goods Risk Initiative (CGRI) specialises in information management, crime analysis and the formulation of strategies and/or actionable crime information products for application by the retail industry in South Africa. The CGRI obtains its funding from its clients. Its purpose is to work with clients, partners and stakeholders to reduce crime in the retail industry. Retail companies enter into a Memorandum of Understanding (MOU) with the CGRI to ensure that daily crime incidents are reported to the company in support of its initiative aimed at reducing crime in the retail industry. It serves about 4 600 retail/wholesale outlets in the country. Each retail/wholesale outlet also appoints a dedicated "Champion" to drive the initiative in his or her company. The information management company obtains its information from its clients and acts as a source of information to its clients, partners and stakeholders. Standard operating procedures (SOPs) exist for information management, crime analysis and the implementation of strategies and actionable crime information products. The security risk information management company is not involved in the implementation of strategies nor does it have any control over criminal activities. Its focus is to provide strategies and/or actionable crime information products to reduce crime and financial losses at its retail/wholesale outlets (CGRI, 2010).

Each retail/wholesale outlet also has its own database to store varying levels of information that affect them. However, their information is generally insurance focused and does not facilitate crime analysis in order to produce preventative measures or enhance police investigations. The CGRI is not prescriptive. It only makes recommendations. The first concern of the retail stores is the safety of customers and its personnel. The second concern is the reduction of losses. The CGRI does not do security risk analysis or security surveys at these outlets (CGRI, 2010).

The CGRI has adopted a centralised approach to information management, crime analysis and the implementation of strategies and/or actionable crime information products. The Head: CGRI and Manager for Member Services and Projects, manage the security risk information within the CGRI (CGRI, 2010).

Business against Crime (BAC) has played a mentoring role to CGRI. Business against Crime's role in the business sector and its communication line with the leadership in the Criminal Justice System (CJS) [Police, Justice and the Private Security Regulatory Authority (PSIRA)] has enabled CGRI to fast-track its relationship with these stakeholders, to the extent that BAC facilitates meetings between CGRI and these stakeholders. The CGRI participates regularly in South African Police Service meetings. It builds relationships with the police stations and clusters (CGRI, 2010).

Crime information management

Clients provide daily crime incident reports to CGRI for crime analysis and formulation of strategies and/or actionable crime information products. Information collection starts at the store. The CGRI relies on the store to provide the information on the crime incident. First information of crime is a telephone call from participating stores. The store follows up on the telephonic report with a relevant incident report for the specific crime and sends it electronically to the CGRI data administrator. The data administrator on the incident management system (IMS) electronically captures it. A reference number is allocated to the incident. Statistical information, geographic information and modus operandi are also provided to the data administrator. No false incidents can be reported as the incidents are coordinated with the police by means of the police case numbers (CGRI, 2010).

Many stores are not prepared to invest in the installation of closed circuit television (CCTV) surveillance camera systems, because their losses do not justify spending that much money on CCTV cameras. They are of the perception that installing CCTV cameras will not prevent an armed robbery from happening. It will only assist the store in identifying the perpetrators. Stores are keener to prevent criminal acts. If prevention is linked to the apprehension of criminals then stores are prepared to invest. On the other hand, certain stores invest a lot of money on the installation of CCTV cameras. They believe that the identification of perpetrators will lead to arrests of perpetrators, which will in turn reduce crimes, which in some cases have proven to be true. Risk managers from the participating stores check their CCTV camera tapes and pass their findings to CGRI who conducts content analysis on the CCTV imagery (CGRI, 2010).

Personnel identity cards are also issued to retail store personnel to help monitor personnel. Personnel identity cards are taken away from personnel when disciplinary action is taken against them. Previously the offending personnel were able to commit an offence in one retail/wholesale outlet and go to work for another outlet without being detected. Personnel cardholders come from merchandising companies, promotion companies, labour brokers, etc. Service providers vet their own staff. CGRI only provides identification cards to all vetted personnel. CGRI coordinates information, develops best practices and gives advice to stores when requested to assist. The company only handles crime information and formulates strategies and or actionable crime information products to combat crime (CGRI, 2010).

Information management, crime analysis and the implementation of strategies and/ or actionable crime information products are handled through CGRI's operating procedures. Clients provide voluntary information. No toll-free public information line is available. Information is not always obtained from external sources. The company discusses its crime incident reports, strategies and/ or actionable crime information products with private security companies, SABRIC, PSI, other stakeholders and the police. CGRI is reactively incident driven. It does not work with covert information. CGRI also works with proactive information, which is passed on to the police to conduct follow-up investigations. SAPS liaises with other government departments for any additional information required by CGRI. However, CGRI does not work for SAPS (CGRI, 2010).

CGRI continuously engages with shop managers and security personnel at the retail/wholesale outlets regarding potential security risks. BAC implemented a project called "Crim Project" (Cash Management Project) to prevent pavement robberies of cash from the retail/wholesale outlets. SABRIC manages this project. Special projects are also managed in a team approach, with participants from the different stores and the police. Of primary concern for the stores is the safety and security of their customers and staff, secondary is the losses they incur. The company contributes towards its projects, which are focused on its crime threats (CGRI, 2010).

Crime information analysis

Crime incident reports are received electronically through the Hi-base automated information system or via e-mails from clients. The information is then transferred onto an analyst notebook. The analyst uses the notebook to evaluate/verify and collate the information. Information is then sent weekly to the risk manager of the relevant outlets for evaluation/verification of facts. Senior crime analysts monitor and verify data integrity. Analysts' programmes were specifically written for junior and senior analysts. Incomplete data is a big problem. The data administrator has to follow up on the incomplete information. Trained data analysts are in-house (home grown). No specialist analysts are used. Analysts' work is only outsourced if a problem occurs with specific types of reports, which need a much more sophisticated analysis. The analyst justifies all information, by verifying the information with the client and the police. The specific software program used by CGRI handles all crime information related to shoplifting, short deliveries of stock, hijacking, cash-in-transit heists, credit card/cheque fraud, burglaries and armed robberies (seven identified crimes). It is not confined to syndicate crimes only. The information is verified with the champion of the company. Problems are often experienced with the completeness of the incident reports and in obtaining case numbers and details of investigating officers from the police (CGRI, 2010).

Although it is not a big problem, retail outlets sometimes do provide incorrect statistical information. One of the big problems is the verification and completion of the data. When the crime incident comes in, the relevant data capturer will review the report, look at it and try to verify the information or try to get the case number and enrich the information (CGRI, 2010).

Information comes in and goes out under classification. The system is not an open system and therefore cannot be accessed by anyone. CGRI's strategy is to collate the data relating to crime incidents, conduct analysis of the information in order to provide accurate and meaningful strategies and/or actionable crime information products to their clients so that they can implement the crime-combating strategies in their stores. It also looks at the various aspects of the crime and decides on what should be done. It identifies problem areas, trends, new modus operandi, etc. and develops new strategies to counter the problems. Analysts also produce profiles of wanted suspects, red alerts and provide police with photos, profiles and any other analytical products when required. CGRI also adds value to the information through criminological research for the purpose of prevention. Analysts also seek clarification, interpretation, draw inferences and provide advice to members. Analysis is done according to standard operating procedures (CGRI, 2010).

Implementation of strategies and actionable crime information products

When an incident of serious crime occurs at a specific retail/wholesale outlet, CGRI sends an SMS message to the cell phones of other clients in the area. This will alert the other clients as to the modus operandi of the particular crime, so that they can harden their targets, in order to prevent it occurring at their outlets. Hotspots (vulnerable areas) are also identified in partnership with the clients, partners and stakeholders. The identified users prepare a hot spot report (vulnerability analysis report) for use. The hot spot report identifies vulnerable areas for attention by SAPS. The South African Police Service (SAPS) deploys personnel according to the hot spot report. Whenever this intervention happens, sharp decrease in crime is noticed at the identified hot spots (CGRI, 2010).

Consumer Goods Risk Initiative attends weekly, monthly, quarterly and annual meetings where strategies and/or actionable crime information products are shared with clients, partners and stakeholders. Hints are given for the prevention of criminal incidents. Consumer Goods Risk Initiative is not involved in the operationalisation of the strategies and/or actionable crime information products. It does not decide on which strategies should be implemented but only recommends the implementation of the strategies (CGRI, 2010).

Security information obtained through security assessments by respective stores are sometimes used to assist in formulating strategies to improve security measures at the store in order to prevent criminal activities. SMS's are used to disseminate information as alerts. Strategies and products are classified by using "confidential" and "restricted" (CGRI, 2010).

The manager responsible for strategies at CGRI visit the store and meet with the risk managers on a monthly basis. At that meeting statistics, trends and the strategies are reviewed. Opportunities and threats are discussed. Best practices are discussed on how to protect the safes, strong rooms, cash office and how to improve alarm systems. Strategies and/ or actionable crime information products are identified and recommended to mitigate the relevant security risk in this regard (CGRI, 2010).

Risk managers from the participating stores sit on the monthly Management Committee (MANCOM) meetings called by CGRI. Information regarding crimes affecting the retail/wholesale industry as a whole is shared with them. Police organised crime units are given information on syndicated criminal incidents for example housebreakings and armed robberies. All Automated Teller Machine (ATM) crimes are handled by SABRIC despite the ATM being situated inside the stores. SABRIC also monitors ATM crimes in terms of modus operandi, etc. SABRIC maintains ATM statistics. CGRI discusses retail crimes with participating store groups and the police (CGRI, 2010).

Different meetings take place with the police and the retail industry. Since the stores are responsible for their own security, they work on their own initiative with the information. They have their own meetings with the police. These meetings with the police are held nationally, provincially and locally. Vulnerabilities are also rated so that police deployment can be enhanced in those areas. Crime prevention awareness is done at shopping centres to overcome incidents of criminality (CGRI, 2010).

Security personnel will only have access to information as deemed necessary by the store management. SAPS only share statistics which are case related. They do not share information on suspects or proactive information. Some of the big security companies are privy to security information from CGRI as crime is considered as a non-competitive issue by them. Security guards at the stores do not have access to information from CGRI. Information provided by security guards is managed by the store management. If necessary it is referred to CGRI. The company communicates directly with the station commissioner at the local police station or the specific cluster commander, organised crime units or the special task force of the police when it encounters crime incidents in progress (CGRI, 2010).

Seventy percent of the participating stores implement strategies and/or actionable crime information products to combat specific incidents. An impact study showed a 46% decrease in crime statistics in 2009. During 2005, the Retail Industry used to undergo an average loss of about R100 000 per incident through armed robberies. Since then, it has decreased to about R30 000 per incident. Losses per incident came down because of cash management strategies. Consumer Goods Risk Initiative makes recommendations to stores on cash management strategies for example; to have as little cash as possible at their outlets, to use as many Cash-in-Transit pick-ups as possible, encourage the use of "dropsafe" drops and to have small cash floats in tills (CGRI, 2010).

Feedback is given to clients on all information of incidents received. All information, strategies and/or actionable crime information products are classified to overcome leakage of information (CGRI, 2010).

Petroleum Security Initiative

The Petroleum Security Initiative (PSI) has been in existence since 2004. PSI is responsible for information management and crime analysis for the South African petroleum industry (participating oil companies). It manages and collates crime incident information collected by its clients, analyses the crime incident information and recommends strategies and/or provides actionable crime information products aimed at mitigating serious crime related to the petroleum industry. This initiative is driven in partnership with five (of the six) participating oil companies. The purpose for PSIs existence is the high level of crimes perpetrated in the petroleum industry and the absence of information management and crime analysis strategies, as well as actionable crime information products. The PSI strategy is to identify the crime drivers, develop strategies to reduce the crimes and to implement preventative measures. Its vision is to reduce the crimes perpetrated against petroleum retailers to an acceptable level. Reference is made to serious and violent crimes including robberies at service stations, hijackings, fuel thefts, truck hijacking and bombings of ATMs. Most of the information focuses on the petroleum industry related retail crimes including Cash-in-Transit (CIT) incidents and ATM crimes perpetrated at petrol station forecourts.

Each oil manufacturing plant or service station operates under individual oil companies. They operate within the policy of the specific oil company for example Engen, Sasol, Caltex, Shell. The specific oil company specifies policy on how the crime information is to be provided to the PSI. The infrastructure for PSI includes a general manager, consequence manager, data capturer and an analyst. Formal training is not provided to their personnel, since many of the incumbents are former police officers who had been exposed to crime information collection and analysis. However, they do provide on the job training on specific issues such as information technology and software training for analytical skills. There are standard operating procedures (SOP) on the expected service delivery requirements. There is no interference with the work of the South African Police Service (SAPS). The PSI is there to support the SAPS in their endeavours to combat and limit crime on premises of petroleum retailers (petrol stations) (PSI, 2010).

Crime information management

The PSI has a 24-hour security incident reporting line. As incidents happen, they are reported through this line. A data capturer who takes down the information of the incident completes an incident report. The incident report includes all relevant details, according to a prescribed reporting format. All the information is captured onto an automated system. There is also a toll-free number for the reporting of crimes in progress, for instance, an armed robbery in progress. If a specific site uses the toll-free number, the system shows who is reporting and from which site the report is emanating. The police are immediately informed of the crime in progress. This number is not for public use.

Sometimes the reporting of incidents by petrol service stations is very sketchy. Some retailers do not report incidents due to competition among retailers. The feeling is that if they do report, they will be penalised by their oil company for not adhering to policy or administrative procedures. If crime incidents are hidden and not reported to the PSI, particulars of the crime incident is eventually obtained from SAPS, media, SABRIC, CGRI or other sources. The PSI is in the process of putting in place a helpline to encourage retailers to report crime incidents without being exposed. This helpline is to enhance reporting of hidden crime incidents. There is no Memorandum of Understanding (MOU) with all stakeholders to share information, due to some entities being disorganised and not equally effective (PSI, 2010).

The PSI uses a Computerised Occurrence Book (COB) with coordinates for all its service sites. It can be used to send simultaneous SMSs to different sites within a particular radius or in general as soon as it receives information on crime incidents. If all retailers report crime incidents, it will improve the crime situation (PSI, 2010).

Business against Crime (BAC) arranges meetings with the leadership of the police and holds bi-monthly meetings with all stakeholders. A representative from BAC also works from the crime support centre at the 10111 police emergency centre. This person is there to liaise directly with all participating industries including the PSI, other stakeholders and the police regarding crime incidents occurring at oil company sites and other places of interest to the other stakeholders. This person represents the BAC (crime support centre). The PSI liaises with the police both nationally and provincially, with SABRIC, cash-in-transit companies and oil companies on a continuous basis. The police work in partnership with the PSI sharing information of commonality (PSI, 2010). Continuous meetings with SAPS cluster commanders and/ or station commissioners positively influences police action. Police enhance operations at hot spot areas identified by the meetings. The enhanced police action reduces crime incidents in that particular hot spot. Annual statistics maintained by PSI showed that whenever there were meetings with the policing clusters, crime levels dropped at the identified clusters (PSI, 2010).

New managers come and go at the various petrol service stations and some new managers are not aware of security procedures on the reporting of crime incidents. Managers have far too many responsibilities and cannot focus solely on security. Their primary focus is to run a business and not to manage crime. They are not adequately trained on security-related issues. Retailers do not train personnel on how to react in the event of armed robberies or how to prevent armed robberies. One big disadvantage is that information could be leaked to perpetrators during the sharing of information. PSI is currently developing a curriculum to assist in the training of site personnel (PSI, 2010).

Crime information analysis

The automated incident report is sent to the analyst for processing. Using the appropriate software the analyst ensures that the information is enriched by using information provided by other sources, such as the police, other oil companies, Consumer Goods Risk Initiative (CGRI), South African Banking Risk Information Centre (SABRIC), the Post Office and South African Insurance Crime Bureau (SAICB), etc. The automated system also does linkage analyses by providing links to other similar information on the system. The information on the system is further enriched by collecting more information to fill the gaps. Once the information is enriched, the analyst then converts it into a daily incident report. The information on the daily incident reports also reflects information of incidents provided by SABRIC on banking and cash-in-transit incidents, which has an impact on threats confronting the oil companies. The collected information is further enhanced with information from criminological research, the media and other open sources, to add value to information on crime incidents. It is a comprehensive document; some days it is up to twenty pages long (PSI, 2010).

The consequence manager is tasked with conducting further investigations at every site in Gauteng where a crime incident had occurred. He will identify the cause/s that led to the occurrence of the incident and determine what has been done and what has not been done. He will also collect additional information, which has not been collected previously, for instance, descriptions of other occupants in the suspect vehicle, colour of vehicles and CCTV images will be viewed for possible suspects. Information on previous incidents is also collected at the specific site. Information on the modus operandi is also obtained. If a specific security weakness is identified, such as poor locking devices and door fittings, guard found sleeping, and involvement of security officials resulting in the criminal incident taking place, the consequence manager will take it up with the retailer and security company employed at the petrol service station (PSI, 2010).

The analyst will add all the new information onto the incident report. The analyst will use all the collected information and provide management with a weekly hot spot report. It will also provide a PSI hot spot forecast on where future incidents may occur as well as identify clusters that are being targeted frequently. Hotspot reports are sent to the same recipients as the incident reports. A third report called the Joint Operational Committee (JOCOM) report is compiled in conjunction with SAPS and other stakeholders. It is a report that deals with crime trends, activities and frequency of crime incidents in the policing clusters where these incidents are most common. This report also serves as a crime threat assessment (CTA) (PSI, 2010).

The crime information analysis process includes collation of the raw information, interpretation, verification and adding value by further investigating the information. The PSI does not have a policy for analysis. All analysis is done using intelligence software similar to that used by SABRIC, banks, mines, SAICB, casinos and tourism. Information is classified at two levels, namely "confidential" and "restricted to specific companies." The analyst is supportive and gives advice whenever needed (PSI, 2010).

Implementation of strategies and actionable crime information products

A daily incident report is sent out electronically. The SMS is used to disseminate the information to sites (petrol service stations) and to all clients including the South African Police Service (SAPS) for implementation. There are about twenty identified users of the daily incident report. It is also provided to SABRIC, CGRI, the Post Office, South African Petroleum Retailers Association (SAPRA) and the different service providers of the various oil companies. The SAPS Gauteng (Provincial Commissioner: Crime Management Centre) also receives the daily incident report, which is disseminated to other policing structures in the province. It is also possible that SABRIC, PSI and companies contracted to the CIT will all report on the same incident to the provincial policing structure for proactive and reactive steps, for example ATM attacks or CIT attacks. All incidents in the daily incident reports, which have already been reported to the SAPS will be part of their daily crime report. Weekly hot spot reports are sent to the same recipients as the daily incident reports. A third report is the JOCOM report. The JOCOM report is not as widely distributed as the other two reports, due to their inclusion of confidential information applicable to specific companies. Because of competition among oil companies, values of losses are not placed in the report that goes to all the recipients. An industry-specific report is also provided to specific oil companies whenever an incident occurs at their sites. This report is also sent to other oil companies and the SAPS. The consequence manager's report is also sent to the specific oil company and the site (petrol service station) where the incident occurred. It is also sent to SAPS (provincial crime management centre) (PSI, 2010).

A monthly analysis report of all incidents is also given to the oil companies only. This report is not for general consumption. Petroleum Security Initiative also participates in big projects run by BAC and SAPS. The company also registers projects if there is a major problem at specific sites (petrol service stations). There are advantages for service stations who implement strategies and/or actionable crime information products provided by PSI. This results in the reduction of crime incidents. In some instances if the retail side does not want to implement certain strategies and/ or actionable crime information products they just ignore the tasking by not acting on it. Those that ignore implementation of strategies and/or actionable crime information products, usually experience a high number of incidents (PSI, 2010).

Whenever there are meetings with cluster commanders/station commissioners and operational interventions follow, incidents at oil company sites show a decrease. On one occasion, there were investigators from police station A in SAPS looking for the same suspects as police station B in SAPS. Police station A did not realise that the perpetrators were being investigated by police station B. There was no linkage analysis. Intervention by security officers of a private security company led to the perpetrators being arrested and linked to cases from police stations A and B (PSI, 2010).

The police provide feedback on progress with investigations being conducted at the different sites. Oil companies also provide feedback on the implementation of strategies. The biggest response comes from individual petrol service stations that liaise directly with PSI. There is no structured way of getting feedback. Formal feedback is given through written reports, emails and informal discussions with specific persons. The analyst also reports and coordinates all successes (PSI, 2010).

AUSTRALIA

The use of private security in crime prevention and law enforcement in Australia has grown to a point where security personnel outnumber police by more than two-to-one. In 2006, there were 52 768 personnel employed full-time in the Australian security industry, compared with 44 898 police members. A decade earlier the police had outnumbered security (Prenzler, Earle and Sarre, 2009). Any person who conducts a business or is employed in a security-related field in Australia is required to be licensed. Each of the six states and territories (New South Wales, Victoria, Queensland, South Australia, Western Australia, Tasmania and Northern Territory) in Australia have separate legislations that cover all security activities. Licensing management varies from state/ territory to state/ territory and is carried out by Police, the Attorney General's Department, Justice Department or the Department of Consumer Affairs. Security officers are not permitted to carry firearms, handcuffs or batons unless they have a legitimate requirement to do so and then only when working and if they have the appropriate sub-class accreditation to their licence (Australian Security Industry Association Ltd, 2011). Presently data indicates that over 5 000 security and investigative businesses are registered in Australia and over 110 000 licences have been issued mainly to individuals (Prenzler et al., 2009).

In Australia, threats and risks are considered as different concepts. A threat is a hazard or a source of risk (criminals, terrorists, etc.) usually measured in terms of intent and capability. A threat also takes into consideration direct impact of natural disasters, for instance, power outages, infrastructure and indirect impact such as fire, looting, civil unrest, etc. Risks are considered as the likelihood of an attack with the most credible impact(s) or consequence on assets. Security risk management therefore involves understanding the threat as part of the objective of determining and implementing counter measures to manage risks (Talbot and Jakeman, 2008).

Security information management
in Western Australia

Private security activities in Western Australia are governed by the Security and Related Activities (Control) Act 1996 and the Security and Related Activities (Control) Regulations 1997. While the term security guard is used by many companies, government bodies and individuals use the term security officer. "Bouncers" are called Crowd Controllers and Store Detectives are called Loss Prevention or Asset Protection Officers. The Western Australian Police Licensing Services (Security) regulates and manages the security industry. The aim is to provide the community of Western Australia with a professional security industry where competency (training), integrity and accountability are maintained at a high standard (Australian Security Industry Association Ltd, 2011).

In Western Australia businesses supplying security products or services must hold the following licences:

- Security Agents Licence that authorises the supply of security officers, security consultants or security equipment services.

- Crowd Control Agent Licence that authorises the supply of crowd control services.

- Inquiry Agents Licence that authorises the supply of investigation services.

Individuals who perform security services need to hold the following non-agent licences:

- Security Officers Licence: to watch, guard and protect property.

- Security Consultant Licence: to investigate and advise on matters relating to the watching, guarding and protecting of property, including security services and equipment sales.

- Security Installer Licence: to install security equipment (does not include installers of security equipment in vehicles, vessels or aircraft).

- Crowd Control Licence: to monitor or control the behaviour of persons, screen persons for entry or remove people from premises. Required for licensed premises, places of entertainment and public or private events or functions (Australian Security Industry Association Ltd, 2011).

Investigator's licence means to legally investigate the conduct of individuals or a corporation or the character of individuals, perform surveillance work or investigate missing persons (Australian Security Industry Association Ltd, 2011). Security information is usually obtained from threat, vulnerability and criticality assessments as well as historical information, management systems and programme activities. This security information is analysed using a risk register. The risk register informs on asset criticality against identified risks and provides a framework from which to allocate the needed physical security resources and funding. The likelihood and consequence of the risk is determined by assessing and defining the risk using descriptive terms (qualitative) and calculated data (quantitative) or a combination of both. Security information on incidents is handled according to an Incident Management and Reporting Guideline. The operationalisation of the security information depends on reports and trends identified through analysis of incidents. The analysis of incidents consistent with other institutional standards is essential in order to maximise the value of the information (Talbot and Jakeman, 2008).

Government departments

Government departments provide policy guidelines and collection plans for the collection of security information. The owners of buildings where government departments are housed, have contracted security service providers. Their functions are mainly directed at access control and taking care of the physical protection systems (PPS). Government departments have their own security heads. They manage security-related activities and conduct workplace investigations on misconduct and other policy-related incidents in respect of the particular government department. These officials are all licensed to perform specific security-related activities. It is the responsibility of all employees and clients to report any information on threats, incidents and vulnerabilities to the security official at the sites. The security officials enter the information into the computer system using a specific template. Software programmes are used to collate the information. Much of this information is handled by the security officials at the respective sites (Australian Government official, 2011a, 2011b).

Security information on crime incidents are referred to the Western Australian Police (WAP). All misconduct and policy-related violations are referred to the regional offices. Different methods are used to collect security information. Open means are most commonly used to collect security information. Networking is also used to gather information. Security managers identify misconducts and vulnerabilities. Risk management profiles determine the types of threats the department is exposed to. The Australian Security Intelligence Organisation Business Liaisons Unit (ASIOBLU), collects security information on threats, analyses it and provides threat assessment reports to government departments in Western Australia. Information is also collected from third parties (Australian Government official, 2011a, 2011b).

Government departments share information among themselves. All information is recorded manually and then transferred to computer systems. Feedback is given according to the information received. A collection unit is tasked to collect any additional information, analyse the information and make recommendations. Actionable information products and threat assessment reports are received for application as security risk control measures. Feedback is then also given on the outcomes of the application of security risk control measures (Australian Government official, 2011a, 2011b).

Western Australian Police

The Western Australian Police (WAP) has a commissioner as head, assistant commissioners as deputies, superintendents in charge of the uniform and detective police divisions, inspectors appointed as district officers, senior sergeants and sergeants in charge of police stations and constables functioning as operational workers. The Australian Crime Commission Corporate Plan 2004 is used as a guiding instrument for the WAP to manage security information on crime (Australian Police official, 2011a, 2011b, 2011c).

The WAP uses the concept "intelligence" rather than "information." This was started in the 1990s when intelligence-led policing first appeared in Australia. It was driven by a number of police commissioners. The local adoption included new accountability structures at a local level, a greater integration of intelligence and investigation to improve daily police efforts through intelligence dissemination. For the purpose of the WAP, the researcher will use the concept intelligence rather than security information (Australian Police official, 2011a, 2011b, 2011c).

The WAP uses overt and covert means of collecting intelligence. Public hotline systems are also used to get intelligence from the public. Intelligence is also provided by third parties. The WAP uses different methods to collect intelligence. Some of the methods include physical surveillance, electronic surveillance, interviews, research, auditing, undercover investigations and forensics. Intelligence is obtained from both internal and external sources. All intelligence is entered into the computer and viewed at local level. The intelligence from the different police stations is viewed by the intelligence group at district level. The different policing units have access to the intelligence according to the classification criteria. Anybody may access any intelligence if he or she has a valid reason to access it. If the reason is invalid, access is denied. The State Intelligence Division also views all intelligence. They share this intelligence at Federal Intelligence level, so that all police states and territories can have access to them (Australian Police official, 2011a, 2011b, 2011c).

Private security companies directly share intelligence with the WAP at the different intelligence levels. National key point companies share intelligence with the State Intelligence Division (SID) at the Critical Infrastructure Security Forum (CISF). These meetings take place four times a month. This sharing is based on scenarios. All intelligence received goes through value rating and security rating, so that the intelligence is sanitised and declassified for sharing (Australian Police official, 2011a, 2011b, 2011c).

The WAP has a specific incident management system (IMS) to manage all reported incidents. Private security companies report all crime incidents to the WAP for investigation. They sometimes assist the WAP with preliminary investigations, but hand over all criminal investigations to the WAP (Australian Police official, 2011a, 2011b, 2011c).

The intelligence is analysed by qualified intelligence analysts at the local district intelligence offices and at the State Intelligence Division and operationalised according to the Commissioner's priority. The intelligence is used to generate actionable intelligence-related products such as profiles, linkage charts, crime pattern analysis and threat assessments for operationalisation. If any further intelligence is needed to enrich the present intelligence, several cells are activated to collect this additional intelligence. Analysts design collection plans for this purpose.

Superintendents do the operationalisation. They do the monitoring and evaluation of the implementation of the actionable intelligence products. Feedback is only given on its success, where necessary (Australian Police official, 2011a, 2011b, 2011c).

Western Australian Private Security Service Providers

Security risk management (SRM) is a subset and an essential part of a broader risk management system. It is simply another management discipline fitting predominantly within the sphere of Risk Management. In Western Australia, more emphasis is placed on investing in Occupational Health and Safety (OHS) of personnel rather than on security risk control measures. This is attributable to the low levels of violent crimes experienced in Western Australia (WA). The collection and analysis of security information and the implementation of security risk control measures is therefore not regulated by the private security environment (Australian Security Service Provider, 2011a–g; Australian Academic, 2011a–e).

Security service providers in Western Australia have individual ways of collecting security information on threats, vulnerabilities and incidents. They also use different collection methods depending on the type of security information they need. Some of the more common methods include physical surveillance, electronic surveillance, interviews, research, audits and forensics. Security companies sometimes hold workshops with interest groups to collect security information. Depending on the nature of the operations, collection plans are specifically structured and used for this purpose. Individual interviews are held, security assessments and critical inspections are conducted and information is collected from third parties. Security service providers do not use collection units to collect security information (Australian Security Service Provider, 2011a–g; Australian Academic, 2011a-e).

In the casino industry, the collection of security information is everyone's responsibility. An information awareness culture is created by the distribution of pamphlets, holding awareness workshops and using a common code of conduct for all employees at the casino. Television screen (LCD) messages are also used to encourage the general public to provide information to specific control points. When campus security guards receive security information they enter such information into their notebooks, obtain statements, prepare written reports and enter the information into a computer system. They handle the information as a policy violation, criminal act or in terms of a contract management plan. Everyone on campus is encouraged to collect security information, as security is everyone's responsibility for example students will inform security if they observe a breach of security or criminal act. Information is managed as a policy violation, criminal act or in terms of a contract management plan (Australian Security Service Provider, 2011a–g; Australian Academic, 2011a–e).

Security information is initially referred to supervisors and then entered into an electronic database. Sometimes security information is received verbally and managed by the immediate supervisors. The threat information is generally referred to the WAP and addressed by the security service provider in consultation with the WAP. Incident reporting information systems (IRIS) are used by campus security to manage security information on incidents. This is usually governed by the policy of the security service provider. The incident information on criminal conduct is generally given preliminary attention and referred to the WAP for investigation. The WAP has the legislative mandate to investigate crime in Western Australia. All incidents on policy violations are sometimes referred to the human resources section of the company for attention or investigated by workplace investigators. All vulnerabilities are handled in terms of a risk management process as determined by the company. It also provides a threat assessment for operationalisation. Private security service providers do not follow a standardised procedure in handling vulnerabilities (Australian Security Service Provider, 2011a–g; Australian Academic. 2011a–e).

The security information is handled in a protected manner. The information can only be accessed if the individual has been permitted to access the required information. Otherwise, access to the information is denied. All security information pertaining to threats and crime in general is discussed with different stakeholders at different forums. There are specific forums that serve the needs of specific security service providers. Some of these forums include: The Critical Infrastructure Security Forum (CISF), Australian Security Industry Association Liaison (ASIAL), Council of Australian Governments (CAG), Industry Security Committee and Trusted Information Sharing Networks (ISCTISN). Security information is shared at these forums on a need to know basis (Australian Security Service Provider, 2011a–g; Australian Academic, 2011a–e).

Many security service providers do not have appointed analysts. Computer software is used in the collation, analysis and generation of actionable information crime products. One such common software used in Western Australia is the incident reporting information systems (IRIS) software, which is used to collate, evaluate and analyse information for application. Security information is analysed only if it can be used. Otherwise, the information is left in the computer to be used as historical information. Investigators or security supervisors are tasked to collect additional information where necessary. They prefer clean information to corrupted information. The casino industry analyses its CCTV and other information as soon as it is received and they notify police immediately of any criminal conduct. It also takes immediate action if the incident is in progress. Data integrity is a problem. Much of the information is not entered onto the system immediately. Sometimes information is not correctly entered into the computer system. Actionable information products and alerts are generated for use by security officials. Feedback on the application of the actionable information products is usually done verbally or in writing (Australian Security Service Provider, 2011a–g; Australian Academic, 2011a–e).

Many security service providers are of the view that they do need to analyse their information as no losses occur at their companies. All crime information is analysed by the WAP and operationalised (Australian Security Service Provider, 2011a–g; Australian Academic, 2011a–e).

SOUTH AFRICA AND AUSTRALIA: A COMPARISON

As much as the researcher is not keen on making comparisons between a developed and a developing country, there are, however, matters of relevance in the management of security information which may be important to compare, as illustrated in table 3.1.

Table 3.1: **Comparisons of security information management in Gauteng, South Africa, and Western Australia**

Gauteng (South Africa)	Western Australia
Security officers are registered by PSIRA	Security officers are registered and licensed by the Western Australian Police
Threats and risks are considered as similar concepts	Threat and risks are considered as different concepts
Security risk management involves understanding the risk as part of the objective of determining and implementing counter measures to manage risks	Security risk management involves understanding the threat as part of the objective of determining and implementing counter measures to manage risks
The terms security guard, store detectives and security risk managers are commonly used in the Security Industry	The term security guard is used by many companies, government bodies and individuals; "bouncers" are called crowd controllers and store detectives are called loss prevention or asset protection officers
Risk assessment or Risk analysis (Probability, Frequency and Impact analysis)	Criticality assessment (Probability, Frequency and Impact analysis)
Security information is analysed by managers using a security officer's incident report	Security information is analysed using a risk register
Security information on incidents is handled by the supervisor at his or her discretion	Security information on incidents is handled according to an Incident Management and Reporting Guideline
Government departments do not provide policy, guidelines and collection plans for the collection of security information	Government departments provide policy, guidelines and collection plans for the collection of security information
Government departments do not share information among themselves nor do they use forums	Government departments share information among themselves and at forums
Collection units are not tasked to collect security information, analyse the information and make recommendations	A collection unit is tasked to collect security information, analyse the information and make recommendations
Concept crime information and intelligence is used by the SAPS	Concept intelligence rather than information is used by the WAP
Private security companies do not directly share information or intelligence with the SAPS at the different policing levels	Private security companies directly share intelligence with the WAP at the different policing levels

Table 3.1: (Continued)

Gauteng (South Africa)	Western Australia
SRM is a model used by the Security Industry to manage risks	SRM is simply another management discipline fitting predominantly within the sphere of risk management
In South Africa more emphasis is placed on investing in security risk control measures	In Western Australia more emphasis is placed on investing in Occupational Health and Safety (OHS) of personnel rather than on security risk control measures
Security officials are not tasked to collect security information on threats, vulnerabilities and incidents	Security officials are tasked to collect security information on threats, vulnerabilities and incidents.
Private security information management companies coordinate and analyse security information on incidents of crime (SABRIC, PSI, CGRI)	Private security information management companies do not coordinate and analyse security information on incidents of crime

CONCLUSION

The grounded theory design assisted the researcher to understand the status quo and the existing problems in security information management. It would be meaningless to draw comparisons between societies with vastly different cultures and levels of crime, especially violent crime. The comparison between South Africa and Australia was used to primarily identify existing standards in both South Africa and Australia in order to enhance the management of security information. The author's intention was to include only those attributes relevant to the collection and analysis of security information and the implementation of security risk control measures. Interviews for this study was conducted under anonymity with academics, senior managers from the police, government departments (with in-house security service infrastructure) and private security service providers in both South Africa and Western Australia. The author did not reveal the names of the interviewees for ethical reasons. One of the advantages of the confidential interviews was that it helped to record more fully the responses of the participants supported by their outward manifestations.

The need for a theoretical framework

OBJECTIVES

- Explain the similarities between Policing and Security Management Models.

- Appraise the need for a theoretical framework for the management of security information.

- Discuss the Crime Pattern Theory and explain its significance to security information management.

- Be able to discuss critically the Security Risk Management Model used in South Africa compared to the International Security Risk Management Model .

INTRODUCTION

The use of information, intelligence and security risk management models (SRMMs) are certainly not new to law enforcement and the security industry. Researchers often refer to Chinese strategist Sun Tzu and his military treatise, *The Art of War*, written 2000 years ago, with references to spies, information, intelligence and security risks (Newburn et al., 2008). Information, intelligence gathering and risk assessments have also been used by many leaders over the centuries to maintain control over their political enemies and business competitors. This chapter introduces some of the different crime information, intelligence and SRMMs and motivates for a theoretical framework for security information management. Although there are many models available within the policing and security environments, these models were specifically chosen for this study, because of their similarities and their common thread to security information management. This chapter discusses the problem-oriented policing model, Compstat model, intelligence-led policing model and the security risk management model (South Africa) currently being used by law enforcement and the security industry and concludes his discussion with the need for a theoretical framework for security information management.

INFORMATION/INTELLIGENCE AND SECURITY RISK MANAGEMENT MODELS

Advances in information management in law enforcement in the 1970s gave rise to modern intelligence practices for law enforcement, to manage crime better in society. The Chiefs of Police from England and Wales in the Baumber Report, made it clear that, "intelligence" has to be understood as something more than simply information. It was also noted that "intelligence" as a modern police concept required that all collected information be put together with others and that analysis be performed in order to produce intelligence. Intelligence has since been accepted in policing as the end product of a process often complex, sometimes physical, and always intellectual, derived from information that has been collated, analysed and evaluated in order to prevent crime or secure the apprehension of offenders (Newburn et al., 2008). The demand for risk-based information is elevating law enforcement to the status of primary producers of crime information. The focus on information and intelligence driven models is to show that law enforcement and private security are shifting from a reactive focus to proactive mechanisms to control crime and non-compliance.

Information Management Models

Problem-oriented Policing Model

Both information or intelligence-led policing and community policing, are seen to be consistent with Goldstein's original concept of "Problem-oriented Policing" (POP). Goldstein's aim was to end the "means-over-ends policing" where he found that too much time and effort was being spent attending to individual incidents, rather than finding strategies to eliminate the causes of these incidents. Since the 1990s the POPs has been adopted by police agencies internationally and on a wide scale in England and Wales (Newburn et al., 2008). The Problem-oriented Policing Model is important for information-led policing. It has opened the eyes of law enforcement and security practitioners to the possibilities of using crime information and analysis to solve crime problems and develop operational strategies to mitigate risks. It looks at a specific and often local nature of a crime problem to determine the nature of the solution. Problem-oriented Policing has yielded many benefits for community policing. Problem-oriented Policing is important for the development of intelligence-led policing, because it has made police managers conversant to the possibility of doing crime information collection and analysis and using the analysis result to design operational strategies to solve crime problems.

Over 60 prominent policing agencies internationally, including the SAPS have associated themselves with the Problem-oriented Policing Model. Police practitioners from these agencies used Eck and Spelman's SARA model, which includes the Scanning, Analysis, Response and Assessment (SARA) methodology to carry out Problem-oriented Policing. SARA involves the following cycle:

- Scanning – identifying recurring problems and how the ensuing consequences affect community safety;

- Analysis – collecting and analysing relevant data on the problem, to reveal ways to alter the causes of the problem;

- Response – seeking out responses that might have worked elsewhere, identifying a range of local options, and then selecting and implementing specific activities that will resolve the problem; and

- Assessment – testing data collected before and after the response phase in order to determine whether the response reduced the problem and, if not, to identify new strategies that might work (Ratcliffe, 2003).

According to Kelling, Pate, Dieckman and Brown (1974), the Kansas City preventive patrol experiment followed the POP approach to study the effectiveness of hotspot policing (place based policing). The study focused its research on the impact of different levels of police patrols in Kansas City. Three controlled levels of routine preventive patrols were compared across 15 beats. In "reactive patrol," officers entered the area only in response to citizen calls for assistance, reducing police visibility in that area. In "proactive," police visibility was increased two to three times its usual level (by adding additional cars for patrol). In the third area, termed "control," the normal level of patrol (one car per beat) was maintained. Information was scientifically collected and analysed using the SARA design. The study found no statistically significant differences in crime in any of the 69 comparisons made between reactive, control and proactive beats. The results from Kansas City suggest that increasing or decreasing levels of random patrol does not have a substantial impact on crime.

The case study in Minneapolis, following the Kansas City preventive patrol experiment in the USA is an example of POP using the SARA design. Over the past two decades, criminologists and police researchers have questioned the effectiveness of uniformed police patrols by conducting a one year is randomised preventive patrol experiment to assess the effect of the increase of police patrols in crime hot spots. Patrol logs and observations were used to validate the duration of patrol presence per day in each hot spot. Findings showed a 13% reduction in crime calls with a more significant reduction in disorder at high crime hot spots. The authors recommended that substantial increases in police patrols will be able to successfully reduce crime and generate more impressive reductions in disorder at high crime hot spots (Sherman and Weisburd, 1995).

Compstat model

The 1980s and the 1990s are seen as periods of innovation for problem and community based crime control solutions, but it was also the period that saw the rapid emergence of Compstat as a crime fighting strategy. Compstat began in the Crime Control Strategy meetings of the New York Police Department (NYPD) in January 1994. Police Commissioner William Bratton, newly hired from the city's Transit Police by mayor Rudy Giuliani, created Compstat with the primary aim of establishing accountability among 76 police commanders. It started by collecting information, analysing the information and implementing strategies to reduce crime. Electronic pin-mapping software and the mainframe computer network were used to manage crime information. It is a process that can be adopted in areas other than policing as well. It has since been adopted and adapted to improve other local government agencies in the USA (Bureau of Justice Assistance, 2013).

The Compstat model which begun about 20 years ago has now become the norm in many police agencies worldwide. In a profession where programs come and go, Compstat has withstood changes in leadership echelons. Today it can be considered as part of the institutional DNA of the police institution. Compstat gives police leadership a daily report on how their departments are performing. We have advanced from a time when police agencies worked with crime data that was six or twelve months old to an age of real time crime data. Crime trends are quickly identified and actions taken to prevent further crime and violence (Bureau of Justice Assistance, 2013).

In practice, the development and use of the Compstat as a data source is a prime example of information led policing. It uses information technology to analyse crime, collate individual crimes in different policing areas and develop crime patterns, which can indicate linkages to show the work of individual offenders, criminal gangs or syndicates and it allows resources to be targeted effectively to deal with crime and criminals (Edwards, 2011). The much publicised crime drop in New York around this time cemented the popular view that Compstat was responsible for making the city safer. Major crime in New York City fell by half from 1993 to 1998 (Ratcliffe, 2003).

When the Compstat crime reduction meetings started in early 1994, maps of crime in New York City were projected onto a wall. This allowed the meeting participants to concentrate on crime hot spots, and pressure was placed on precinct commanders to address emerging hot spots. Within Compstat the application of the term intelligence is slightly at odds with how the word is more commonly used. Within the Compstat framework, intelligence more frequently refers to mapped data and is more akin to information than the integrated crime intelligence. The crime reduction mechanism of Compstat involves four principles:

- timely and accurate intelligence

- effective tactics

- rapid deployment

- relentless follow-up and assessment (Ratcliffe, 2003)

Compstat was associated with a significant reduction in crime in New York City and as a result the strategy rapidly spread throughout the world, fuelled by the media, public and law enforcement enthusiasm. Bill Bratton implemented Compstat in the Los Angeles Police Department (LAPD), John Timoney brought Compstat to Philadelphia and updated it in Miami, Gary McCarthy expanded Compstat significantly in Chicago, and Edmund Hartnett brought it to Yonkers, New York New South Wales Police introduced Compstat under the heading "Operation and Crime Review" (OCR). It was based on the Compstat model. The operational room was located in Sydney, the capital city. From August 2001 – June 2004, the Queensland Police Service in Australia used the Compstat model and reduced crime at a cost of AU\$ 1 000 000 (Bureau of Justice Assistance, 2013).

According to research findings, in practice, the general aim of most of the Compstat sessions is to address street crimes, such as robberies and assaults, and property crimes, such as vehicle theft and burglary. Compstat has not been widely applied to more esoteric crime activity, such as organised crime or transnational crime, and it has not been applied to broader areas that community policing may address (Ratcliffe, 2003). Leaders also realised that Compstat should not only analyse the performance of precinct commanders, so they began including detectives and representatives from other specialised units. The biggest changes brought about by Compstat is on information sharing (Compstat helped to facilitate the flow of information), decision-making (commanders were given greater authority) and organisational culture (the police became more creative, flexible, and better equipped to manage risk) (Bureau of Justice Assistance, 2013).

The Compstat process was implemented by the SAPS in 2000. Prior to 2000, the SAPS used Statistical Analysis and crime pattern analysis (CPA) to compare crime figures. Managing the growth and improvement of the Compstat process is challenging, especially with regard to technology and software changes. Computer hardware, operating systems and mapping software change at a very rapid pace. The department does not adopt every software revision and operating system upgrade. Eventually, some changes do take place. In some instances, new hardware may not support older software and vendors may discontinue technical support for their older products. An ongoing assessment of changing technology and its impact has become a routine part of managing the Compstat process (Goldsmith et al., 2000).

Intelligence management models

The National Security Intelligence Management Model

People with privileged access to an organisation's systems and resources are a serious threat by way of both communication intelligence (COMINT) and human intelligence (HUMINT). These threats are in existence in almost all organisations today. The consequence of insider threats includes financial losses, disruption of business operations and harm to individual employees and customers. The insider threat revolves in response to changing technology, social, economic and cultural factors. Depending on the particular organisation its policies and procedures, it is not always easy to collect all the required information/intelligence needed to define insiders. Risk management in organisations should directly address the insider threat by implementing security controls with a focus on behaviour and technology (Garcia, 2008).

According to Fischer et al., (2008: 31) and Bosch, (1999: 4) "Security implies a stable, relatively predictable environment in which an individual or group may pursue its ends without disruption or harm and without fear of disturbance or injury." In the security environment, "private security" includes efforts by individuals and organisations to protect their assets against loss, harm or reduction in value, due to threats. These assets may include people, immovable property, business rights, information, company image, operational strategies, contracts, agreements, and policy. Tragic events such as the September 11, 2001 terrorist attacks in New York and Washington and the more recent terrorist hostage situation in 2013, at a shopping mall in Kenya, and the convictions of individuals in connection with terrorism-related offences in the United States of America and the United Kingdom, demonstrate the need for effective "national" security intelligence by governments. In the light of the challenges posed to national security in the above countries, the need for management of national intelligence activities is imperative (Fischer et al., 2008).

The National Security Intelligence Management Model encompasses a series of steps called the intelligence cycle. The cycle begins with the need for intelligence. Usually it takes the form of a general question from an intelligence customer (one who requests the intelligence), such as "how porous are our South African borders?" Then comes the planning phase, that is how the other proponents of the cycle will address the problem. Collectors will have to be tasked to gather missing bits of information. Analysts will have to be assigned to do research and report on the porous nature of the South African borders. The cycle then proceeds to the gathering of information. Media articles from towns on the South African borders will have to be acquired. Communication intelligence (COMINT) will have to be obtained from the communication media servicing the border towns. Human intelligence (HUMINT) will have to be obtained from persons with knowledge of the South African borders and its activities. The gathered information has to be analysed by an intelligence analyst. Foreign language material has to be translated. Encrypted signals need to be decrypted by language specialists. Film or digital signals should be translated into visible imagery. Responses from the HUMINT sources have to be validated and organised into a report format. The newly collected and processed information should be used to create intelligence during the analysis phase. The intelligence analyst should create outcome scenarios based on the current situation at the borders, generate profiles of borders and security incidents and assess the likely recurrence of such incidents. The analysis phase also includes a peer and supervisory review of the end product. The end product should be disseminated to the client in a written report (electronically) or a briefing. A transition for new requirements or needs is established, and a new cycle begins (Clark, 2010). In South Africa, the security intelligence cycle was used for national security reasons prior to 1995. During this period, private security in South Africa is assisted by the South African Police Service (SAPS) with national security intelligence to provide security at national strategic installations.

Intelligence-led policing

Even with the ability to spread new ideas and innovation throughout the policing world at the click of a mouse, there is still a lack of clarity among many law enforcement officials and security practitioners as to what intelligence-led policing is, what it aims to achieve, and how it is supposed to operate. Intelligence-led policing (also known as "intelligence-driven policing") had its origins in the United Kingdom (UK) in the 1990s, when traditional reactive methods of policing failed to cope with the rapid changes in globalisation which had increased opportunities for transnational organised crime. The National Intelligence Model (NIM) of the United Kingdom used four elements for its tactical tasking in the implementation of intelligence-led policing. These elements include:

- targeting offenders (especially targeting of active criminals through overt and covert means);

- the management of crime and disorder hot spots;

- the investigation of linked series of crimes and incidents; and

- the application of preventative measures, including working with local partnerships to reduce crime and disorder (Ratcliffe, 2003).

In the late 1990s intelligence-led policing was implemented in Australia, driven by a number of police commissioners. The local adoption included a new accountability structure at local level, a greater integration of intelligence and investigation and improved targeting of daily police efforts through intelligence dissemination (Ratcliffe, 2003). The Intelligence-led Policing Model is used when normal investigations do not produce the desired results. The target is usually unaware of the fact that the police are engaged in an investigation against him or her. The production of intelligence in intelligence-led policing has different stages, which includes direction to collect intelligence, evaluation, collation, analysis, dissemination and feedback. These form part of the intelligence cycle with a regular flow, whereby disseminated intelligence triggers operational responses, which in turn produces new information to be fed back to the intelligence unit for new analysis (Newburn et al., 2008; Ratcliffe, 2009).

The South African Police implemented intelligence-led policing in 1995. It was implemented to deal with organised crime syndicates. Crime analysts were used to identify problem crimes, using the crime pattern analysis (CPA) matrix, generated through the automated crime reporting process known as the Crime Administration System (CAS). Once a crime problem, for example street robberies, had been identified, the crime analysis unit would be tasked to collect information on previous incidents of street robberies, the arrested persons, victims and the outcome of the adjudication process, using the docket analysis strategy. Intelligence is gathered on the associates of the previously arrested street robbers, their different memberships and structures. This is done using overt and covert techniques to collect information/ intelligence. The intelligence unit uses this information to develop a linkage analysis chart or an Association Network Analysis Chart (ANAC). The ANAC brings together all the associates of the identified perpetrator/s. It also links the perpetrator/s to specific activities and institutions. The ANAC assists the investigator to conduct a money or paper trail in organised crime investigations. The crime intelligence unit is an organisational structure with personnel who are skilled in the collection and analysis of crime information/intelligence. The analysis function will include the processing of a product for use by decision-makers. The aim was to target the criminal and not the crime. This is because research has shown that a small percentage of repeat offenders (recidivists), commit a large amount of crime (NCIS, 2000).

Security risk management models

According to Blyth and Kovacich (2006), risk management involves taking steps to reduce risks to an acceptable level and maintaining that level of risk. It is a subset and essential part of a broader risk management system. Security risk management is simply another management function fitting predominantly within the sphere of risk management. Other disciplines involved in security risk management include emergency response, business continuity, occupational health and safety (OHS), financial management and project management. If we look at security as a state of being protected from hazards, danger, harm, loss or injury, it also includes elements of protection from national disasters and concepts of organisational resilience (Talbot and Jakeman, 2008). Security service providers should be made aware that the design and implementation of security risk management systems will depend on an organisation's environment, legal obligations, social expectations, needs, objectives, products, services, processes and practices.

International model

Security risk management is making the most efficient before-the-loss arrangement for an after-the-loss continuation of business. Security risk management allows risks to be managed in a logical manner, using long held management principles (Fischer et al., 2008). In 2009, the International Standards Organisation (ISO) propagated the use of ISO 31000. This international standard puts forward principles (a risk philosophy), framework and process. The generic framework provides for the identification, analysis, evaluation, treatment, monitoring, and communication of risk. The security risk management process has three distinct stages, commencing with the establishment of the context, followed by risk assessment and concluding with risk treatment. The purpose of the ISO 31000 is not to enforce uniformity of security risk management systems, but rather to specify the security risk management process in any given organisation (Smith and Brooks, 2013).

Establish the context

The importance of establishing the security risk management context fully and comprehensively cannot be understated and stakeholders should be engaged to identify the strategic context, security risk management context and organisational context (Talbot and Jakeman, 2008). The focus of the context should be on the interrelationship between the different functions and departments in an organisation, business enablers such as leadership, strategic knowledge, management and understanding of legal aspects of the business to business accruement (Smith and Brooks, 2013). Although security risks are limited to three common categories, such as personal, property and liability it is still important to establish the correct context. It is important to note that a security manager is first and foremost a security manager, and then a security practitioner. Security risks are associated with virtually every imaginable activity (Pupura, 2013).

Security risk assessment

The security risk assessment process includes risk identification, risk analysis and risk evaluation.

Identify risks

According to Fay (2006), security risks of concern to organisations include terrorism, political conflict, military operations, harm from criminals and disaster management. Security risk identification normally arises from the defined context, which is informed by the threat, vulnerability and criticality assessments, as well as historical information management systems and programme activities. During the security risk assessment we need to ask the questions what, when, where, how and who for clarity (Talbot and Jakeman, 2008).

Analyse risks

The first step in the security risk analysis process is the identification of threats and vulnerabilities. Many threats in business are important to security, but some are more obvious than others are. The key is to consider the specific vulnerabilities in an organisation (Fischer et al., 2008). The logistical aspects relating to procurement, implementation and ongoing maintenance of physical protection systems (PPS) such as alarm systems, fencing, guards and the installation and maintenance of technical solutions, can present significant immediate and ongoing costs to an organisation. A risk register is one of the most practical ways used by security service providers for the cataloguing of identified risks and measuring the costs of preventing their occurrence. It benchmarks the asset criticality against identified risks. It also provides a framework from which to allocate physical security resources and infrastructure funding (Talbot and Jakeman, 2008). It is necessary to conduct security risk analysis exercises regularly to determine a company's specific exposure to specific crime threats. The security risk analysis will point out weaknesses, which will assist the security risk manager to establish the relative manageability of the identified security risk (Fay, 2006). Regular analysis of security risks will also help to determine if the security practitioner has the ability to identify risks as well as identify the physical opportunity for crime and whether he or she has the ability to prepare recommendations for management to take a decision.

Evaluate risks

After physical protection system objectives have been established and a new upgraded design has been developed, it is necessary to evaluate the effectiveness of the design in meeting the objectives. The evaluation can be done using the quantitative or qualitative methods or a combination of both methods (Garcia, 2008). One of the most common security risk evaluation techniques involves determining likelihood and consequence. Usually these metrics are defined using one or more of three methods:

- Qualitative – using descriptive terms and phrases to assess and define risk

- Quantitative – using historical or calculated data

- Combined qualitative/quantitative – using numbers to provide comparative assessment of likelihood, consequence and/or risk (Talbot and Jakeman, 2008).

Treat risks

Once the security probability and criticality analysis has been completed and the security problems have been identified and ranked in importance, the security manager in cooperation with other members of management must decide on how the security risks should be treated (Fischer et al., 2008). Security risk response and controls include a range of security measures. The objective is not only to eliminate risks but also to reduce risks to the point where it is as low as reasonably practicable. Regardless of the organisation's or individual's risk tolerance levels, the following risk treatment principles are important:

- do not accept unnecessary risks;

- accept risk only if the benefits outweigh the costs;

- risks should be managed at the point where it occurs Talbot and Jakeman, (2008); and

- risks may be treated by using different alternatives such as risk avoidance, risk reduction, risk spreading, risk transfer, and self-assumption of risk (Fischer et al., 2008; Fay, 2006; and Smith and Brooks, 2013).

Security risk management plan

The purpose of a security management plan is to prevent an adversary from successfully executing a malicious act against an organisation/ entity. The primary functions of such plan should include elements such as detect, deter, delay, deny, respond and recover. The establishment of a security risk management plan provides an organisation with executive support and impetus to manage risk (Garcia, 2008). A security risk management plan should incorporate strategies to reduce the cost of risk management relative to identified threats and to assign the most appropriate risk treatment to each identified risk. A key element of the design of security risk management involves the application of treatments that (in priority order) involves the objectives to deter, deny, delay, detect, respond and recover against a potential threat.

- Deter: A deterrent factor is a device or barrier that controls unauthorised access into a facility. It displays its inherent asset protection capabilities against potential criminals attempting unauthorised entry. Deterrent factors can take many forms, such as fencing, signposts, visible guards, or a barking dog. They may deter an unauthorised access to an asset.

- Deny: The denial of access to unauthorised parties to an asset is another mechanism used to promote security.

- Delay: A delaying factor is a barrier or scenario that provides time for another protective measure to take effect, should unauthorised access to an asset occur.

- Detect: Detection may occur in a variety of ways including alarms, system logs, direct observation, patrols, CCTV or signs of attempted entry.

- Respond: A response must be consistent and appropriate with the level of threat detected against the asset.

- Recovery: Recovery is the final barrier to mitigate the long-term consequences of any attack by returning to desired levels of capabilities as quickly as possible (Talbot and Jakeman, 2008).

South African model

Security service providers in South Africa use different SRMMs (processes) to manage security risks in their environment. The different models are used as a management tool for the collection of security risk information, conducting security risk analysis and implementing appropriate security measures. Many risk simulation packages on the market has made this possible. These packages are good to aid in the decision-making process, but should not be seen as a solution to security risk management problems. Many security service providers in South Africa also use a practical SRMM (process) to manage security risks in their environments. Many security practitioners who studied Security Management at University of South Africa are currently applying this practical Security Risk Management Model developed by the former Programme Security Management at Technikon SA (renamed the Department of Security Risk Management (DSRM) after the merger with University of South Africa in 2004 and again renamed Programme Security Management at the time of the merger in 2009 with the Department of Criminology). The primary aim of the model is to manage security risks confronting organisations/entities, whose risks are largely of a criminal nature. The model focuses on the identification, measurement (establishing probability), and analysis of vulnerabilities (security measure weaknesses) that lead to the exploitation of opportunities. The SRMM is based on the following process:

- Identifying the problem posed by crime;

- Considering the security policy and mandate in relation to the problem;

- The orientation phase;

- The risk analysis exercise;

- The comprehensive security survey;

- Security risk control measures;

- Return on investment;

- The crime risk management report; and

- Implementation, evaluation and maintenance of security measures (Rogers, 2008).

Other Security Risk Analysis Models are also used to calculate the annual cost of losses. One such Crime Risk Analysis Model, used to determine the frequency of losses and the frequency of exposure to specific risks, is that of Fay (2006). This model tests the probability, impact and frequency of specific criminal acts. This model tests the following common questions:

- What is the probability of a criminal act being committed?

- Is the probability of the occurrence unknown, unlikely, likely or certain?

- What will be the impact of such a criminal act in terms of costs of replacement, repair, lost productivity, forfeiture of business opportunity, clean-up, litigation, damage to reputation and undermining of customer goodwill?

Frequency is different from probability, in that the police will be able to provide the security manager with a record of all such occurrences for the period in question (daily, weekly, monthly yearly or longer).

According to Fay (2006), it is important for management to be aware of the relative manageability of crime as a risk. Manageability is the capacity to reduce the probability and/or impact of a risk. The principle methods of managing risks include the following:

- Avoiding the risk by removing the target. Laptop theft can be avoided entirely by choosing not to provide laptops to employees. A trade secret, such as the formula for a popular soft drink, can be kept in a high-security vault. Some businesses avoid crime-related risks by choosing not to operate in high-crime areas.

- Reducing the risk by decreasing the target. A convenience store robbery loss can be reduced by placing all cash receipts above a designated amount in a floor safe. The store's shoplifting risk can be reduced by placing high-value merchandise in locked cabinets and easily concealed high-demand items, such as packets of cigarettes, behind the cashier's counter.

- Diffusing the risk involves the use of barrier systems such as perimeter fences, access control, and intrusion detection equipment such as card readers and CCTV, locks, safes and vaults; and standard control procedures such as property removal passes and inventory counts.

- Transferring the risk is possible by purchasing insurance or by increasing prices so that the purchasers of the product or service pay for the losses. Another technique is to outsource risk-heavy functions to another party. An example is the transfer of liability when an employer replaces an in-house guard force with a contract guard force. If misconduct by a contract guard causes a serious accident, the employer may be able to escape liability under the terms of the contract.

- Accepting the risk is also an option. Management may decide that a particular risk is worth the gamble, or that the cost of loss does not justify the cost of prevention. Another deciding factor may be the intractability of the risk (that is, that despite the best efforts, the risk cannot be controlled to an acceptable degree).

A THEORETICAL FRAMEWORK IS NECESSARY

Theory is inescapable, because the security industry does not operate in a vacuum. It operates in a dynamic environment confronting crime problems and losses, which are complex and changing all the time. Our action on managing the activities of security is premised on assumptions and expectations about how the world works and how others should behave and act as security service providers. Over the last decade-and-half, private security officials in South Africa have developed and increased their skills and body of knowledge. Some of this development has been necessitated by the increasing use of new (security) technology, equipment and growing managerial sophistication within this specialised field of expertise (Minnaar, 2005). Many have been employed as security officials at various government departments, that is, not confined to the "private" security sector. They safeguard and protect government assets just as in the private sector (Irish, 1999: 1). Much of this knowledge, skills and technology is theoretically founded. The theories they embody are not absolute or reliable, hence they are available for critical scrutiny if they are to be understood and improved (Tilley, 2009).

Secondly, theory will be based on institutional policies and practices used in the management of security information. Private security service providers commonly use the SRMMs as the underlying theoretical framework to identify security risks in organisations being protected (Fischer et al., 2008). Based on the identification and analysis of the risks confronting an organisation, security measures are often reinforced to adequately protect a vital portion of an organisation/entity. This model is focused entirely on identifying risks, with very little emphasis being placed on day-to-day incidents, threats and vulnerability information. Theory is needed to guide the policymaker and the security practitioner. According to Tilley (2009), well-tested and well-structured theories form the basis for informed planning and implementation. To mould people to conform to management's expectations and what management needs to do when there is failure to conform, should be the thrust of institutional policies.

Thirdly, theory has to do with values and the implementation of policy and practice in the security environment. Our every action is premised on assumptions and expectations on how the security industry operates and how its officials implement policy and procedures in practice. We have to depend on these assumptions to get by in managing the private security environment. Everything is taken for granted based on existing theories such as the routine activity theory, opportunity theory, rationale choice theory and the crime pattern theory. The routine activity theory makes us assume that all security service providers conduct activities in a similar way. The opportunity theory makes us assume that management keeps abreast with the ever-changing technological advancement to cope with environmental changes. The rationale choice theory makes us assume that management always makes a rationale choice by carefully planning interventions after weighing up all the possible risks (Edwards, 2011). The crime pattern theory describes and explains the geographical distribution of crime and incidents of policy violations. It does this by looking at the routine activities of an individual/s and the awareness spaces that suspected offenders need to conduct an illegal activity. These awareness spaces relate to the routine routes that people usually take to conduct their daily activities. This can be at the individual's business office, home, school, recreation centre, etc. These awareness spaces present opportunities for the offender to strike at his or her target. They will provide likely times for the offender to strike. This crime will tend to be geographically concentrated in times and places that lie within the offender's awareness space, where there are ample targets for crime. Some places also act as crime generators or crime attractors. These places create the opportunities for the commission of crime or violation of policy. Crime attractors are those places, which are known suitable targets for crime, which are well known to the offenders for example, liquor taverns act as generators or attractors of crime. An example of an incident of policy violation may include finding a spot to sleep on duty, where there is no CCTV coverage or out of the sight of passers-by. The relationship between the opportunities theory and the crime pattern theory is very obvious from the above. Crime pattern theory is used for prevention efforts and geographical profiling of prolific offenders whose likely routine activities can be gauged from the distribution of the offences (Tilley, 2009).

CONCLUSION

This chapter discussed the similarities between the information, intelligence and security risk mitigation models used by law enforcement officials and security practitioners in combatting crime and mitigating security risks. Cyber-crime, property-related crimes, corruption, organised crime and transnational organised crime, require law enforcement and private security to respond with information/ intelligence management strategies. Information/ Intelligence and security risk management strategies are central to the task of preventing crime and reducing losses. Data related to the vulnerability of a target presents the opportunity to address the exploited weaknesses of an asset/victim. The information/intelligence and SRMMs discussed have been effectively used by the author to design and develop a theoretical framework for security information management.

CHAPTER 5

Security information management model

OBJECTIVES

- Discuss the problems that gave rise to a security information management model.

- Reconstruct the model for the collection and analysis of security information and the mitigation of security risks.

- Apply the model for the management of security information, describing each stage.

- Formulate a policy framework for the management of security information.

INTRODUCTION

Security information collection first emerged in the mid-1950s. From then onwards the extent, complexity and detail of security information collection, analysis, interpretation and utilisation changed dramatically and developed in many different ways. These changes and developments in the field of security management, gave rise to the design and development of a security information management model (SIMM). All stakeholders in an organisation need to be informed of these changes and developments, in order to ensure that they are aware of the importance and impact of security information in their overall work environment. Contextually, security management will derive the most significant benefits from the SIMM, which should be integrated into the organisations' existing functional processes. Security information management should be seen as part of the existing functional processes of an organisation. Incidents, threats and vulnerabilities have the potential to affect an organisation's assets negatively. Information on these incidents, threats and vulnerabilities are important to security. It is therefore necessary for this security information to be managed effectively and efficiently, so that correct decisions can be made on the implementation of security risk control measures. A SIMM is important for the management of security information. This chapter will discuss the design and development of the SIMM.

DEVELOPMENT OF A SECURITY INFORMATION MANAGEMENT MODEL

No specific SIMM currently exists for the collection and analysis of security information on security incidents, threats and vulnerabilities, and for the implementation of appropriate security risk control measures to reduce crime, increase detection rates and prevent losses in organisations.

Justification for the Model

Collection of security information

According to the respondents, no policy framework exists for the collection of security information. In general, security information is not collected according to the threats and vulnerabilities confronting an organisation. Most of the information is randomly collected by security managers, investigators and supervisors. This type of collection is done mainly by using technical and human methods. No standardised framework is in place to guide security personnel on the collection of security information. None of the respondents mentioned an organisational security strategy, security plan, threat assessment document, VA document or a collection plan on the steps followed to collect security information. It is indicative that security information is arbitrarily collected with no objectives and outcomes to guide the process.

The handling of the collected security information should be streamlined to be less cumbersome, so that information may be immediately operationalised. Presently, more emphasis is placed on collecting security information on incidents than on threats and vulnerabilities. This is confirmed by the fact that most information is collected from victims and complainants involved in incidents. Security personnel are more accustomed to the SRMM. There is this confusion of mixing the processes used for security risk management with that of security information management.

Only fifty per cent of the respondents in this study indicated that they use automated systems to store information. This is an indication that about fifty per cent use other means than computers for the storage of security information. The protection of information should be based on trust rather than creating mistrust between management and grassroots security personnel. This is based on the assumption that grassroots security personnel come into daily contact with personnel and clients and serve as the eyes and ears of management.

Fear and victimisation are seen as the biggest intimidating factors in the collection of security information. Personnel are reluctant to provide security information in the workplace. Many workplace investigations are not successfully concluded because personnel are reluctant to make statements implicating colleagues. In view of existing problems in the collection of security information, it can be assumed that management in the security business is not creating a culture of information awareness.

Legal restrictions on the collection of intelligence is an impediment for private security service providers. They are unable to collect intelligence on threats and incidents of crime. Even if intelligence comes to their attention, they need to refer the intelligence to SAPS or to the National Intelligence Coordination Committee in order for legally mandated intelligence agencies to attend to it. The collection of security information sometimes infringes on the rights of people. The handling of the collected security information is not standardised and streamlined which results in information overload. Security information is shared on a need to know basis. Not all information is made available to law enforcement and law enforcement does not make information readily available to security service providers.

In most instances, security officials have insufficient knowledge on the collection of security information. Many security officials do not have skills to identify security-related information. Some of the security officials are unable to record information or statements as a result of poor communication and writing skills. Security officials do not receive training on how to collect security information by using different collection sources, methods and techniques.

Security incident information sometimes suffer as a result of under-reporting and is also highly variable in its accuracy and quality, particularly in the way addresses and locations are geographically referenced. In some instances the inaccuracies may be as a result of the interpretation put on the information by the recording official.

Analysis of security information

According to the respondents, no policy framework exists for the analysis of security information. The quality of security information received for analysis will determine the results of the analysis, which may take the form of a recommendation for strategy, security protection systems or actionable information products to address a specific threat. Most of the security information received by security supervisors for decision-making is insufficient, unreliable and inaccurate. In many instances, this information is used for decision-making by security management without any form of enrichment. These decision-makers are mainly security officers or security supervisors with no analysis training or qualifications. Security information only goes through an analysis process if the security service provider has an analysis capability. Owing to the cost of such infrastructure, very few security companies have a qualified analysis capability. Hence, very little security information goes through the analysis process.

The organisational strategic direction, the security plan, threat assessment, VA, incident pattern analysis (IPA) and the needs of clients ought to be considered for the purpose of analysis. The types of analysis results that analysts provide clearly show that this is not the case. It appears as though security service providers generate more actionable information products, reports and security assessments than strategies to reduce crime, increase detection rates and prevent losses. This function of analysis needs more innovation and cognitive thinking. In addition, an information overload problem indicates that information is collected at random and given for analysis. It would seem that the trend is to analyse all information that is received to prepare counter measures even though there is no threat present. This, to the knowledge of the researcher, is a waste of money, human resources and technology as the security information that is being analysed is not key to the organisation's needs. The key information need should be part of the security plan or specifically requested by management. The fact that there is a need for qualified analysts, computer equipment and analytical software, one can safely assume that security service providers find it difficult to reduce crime, increase detection rates and prevent losses.

Many organisations do not make use of computer technology, computer hardware and software for the purpose of analysis. Only some of the big organisations with qualified analysts in their employ use the automated analysis function. Only in exceptional and sensational incidents will security information be outsourced to qualified analysts for analysis reports. Many organisations have found this to be more beneficial and cost-effective than investing in an in-house analysis capability.

Certain organisations with analysis capability sometimes have problems with the integrity of their information. In many instances, the information is insufficient, unreliable and inaccurate. The security information is not tested to determine if it meets the key information needs of the analyst. Analysts experience problems in obtaining missing information in the absence of a collection capacity. In most cases, the analysis results are not directed at addressing specific threats or vulnerabilities. The analysis process does not consider the organisation's threat assessment, VA and IPA. In many instances, actionable information products are often found to be irrelevant, unreliable or not timely. Management sometimes undermines and generalises the analysis results before disseminating it. There is no ongoing communication between analyst and user of analysis results. Analysts do not disseminate analysis results. Analysis results take too long. In many instances, the analysis results are not relevant to the security risk prevalent at the time. Management does not do much to manage data integrity and quality control of the analysis results before passing it on to end users for implementation.

Analysis is not done by qualified, experienced personnel. Management should not undermine analysis results. There should not be mistrust between management and lower level security personnel. Management should not generalise analysis results or interfere with the analysis function. Security information must be analysed in a structured way. Regular communication should take place between analyst and end user of the analysis result. The end user of the analysis result should be allowed to request additional analysis on the result. Data integrity of analysis results should not be compromised. A data analysis centre should be established to monitor incidents. Dissemination should also take place formally by means of reports.

Implementation of security risk control measures

According to the respondents, there is no policy framework for the implementation of security risk control measures. The analyst's findings and recommendations are generalised by management to downplay the seriousness of the threat or vulnerability. Different methods are used for dissemination and feedback. This may seriously compromise the protection of the information and may result in information leaks. The implementation of security risk control measures is not needs driven. It does not take into consideration the reduction of crime, increasing the detection rates and preventing losses. The fact that communication is not encouraged between the analysts and the end user indicates that the implementation of the security risk control measure is not monitored and evaluated.

The implementation of specific security risk control measures by security service providers are quantitatively driven in terms of cost. The qualitative design of the security risk control measure to deter, detect, delay and respond to the intruder is not taken into consideration. If funding is not forthcoming from the organisation being protected, then either the security information to enhance the security measures is shelved or a more cost-effective measure is implemented.

Security risk control measures take the form of prevention measures (more body and property searches during access control), disciplinary action and criminal prosecution. Very seldom do they take the form of PPS, strategies and actionable crime information products. Security risk control measures are implemented without giving due consideration to the reduction of crime, increase in detection rates and the prevention of losses. The implementation of security risk control measures is not needs driven. Clients are unwilling to pay for additional resources to implement security risk control measures that are not needs driven.

In many instances, there is no communication between the analyst and the security official responsible for the implementation of the security risk control measures. The intended users are not always in a position to operationalise the security risk control measures, as the measures are sometimes outdated. If the services of a qualified analyst is used the results and recommendations are in some instances undermined and generalised by management, to downplay the seriousness of the threat or vulnerability. Many of the personnel do not have the experience to implement security risk control measures. They are not trained to implement security measures. In many instances, the resources are insufficient to implement analysis results.

Management seldom receives feedback. Management receives much of the feedback informally regarding the progress of implementation. Line management does not monitor and evaluate the implementation of the security measures. There is no evaluation of the implementation of the security risk control measures. Security risk control measures do not include implementation strategies. There is a need to have a structured way of implementing security risk control measures.

Security information management

Based on the abovementioned reasons, the researcher recommends a SIMM to manage security information in organisations. The model should be flexible and user friendly. It should comprise concepts associated with security information management (chapter 2), a framework inclusive of the three phases (chapter 5), and the process (chapter 6). The model should be based on a common body of knowledge for security information management specifically suited for the security industry. It should introduce a new dimension to the security industry in the sphere of collection and analysis of security information on security incidents, threats and vulnerabilities and the implementation of security risk control measures to reduce crime, increase detection rates and prevent losses. The model should not aim to enforce uniformity of security information management systems, rather to specify the security information management process in an organisation.

The model should include a framework comprising the collection phase analysis and implementation phases. The collection phase should introduce the security practitioner to strategic planning, organisational security strategy, a security plan and a collection plan. These plans if implemented accordingly will help manage security information effectively and efficiently within a specific budget. In the analysis phase, it should introduce the security practitioner to the organisational security strategy, security plan, qualified analysts' capabilities, key information needs, tasking to collect missing information, evaluation and interpretation and analysis results. Threat assessment, VA and IPA documents are all documents that are relevant to the analysis phase. These are "real-time" live documents, which can be continuously used by all levels of the security industry. The implementation of the security risk control measures phase should reflect on the strategic objectives, design and the implementation of security risk control measures.

This security information management framework relates to the collection of security information on security incidents, threats and vulnerabilities. As such, it should include all crime and noncompliance related risks. The analyst should be responsible to conduct a threat analysis, vulnerability analysis and IPA to prepare an assessment of threats, vulnerabilities and incidents. The cycle should include three important stages: the timely collection of security information on incidents, threats and vulnerabilities; the rapid analysis of security information; and the designing of strategies, actionable crime information products and PPS to deter, detect, delay, and respond to an adversary.

The SIMM should be entrenched in a policy framework supported by standard operating procedures for implementation. Threat assessment, VA and IPA documents should be discussed with the security head. All three of these documents will help guide the security head of an organisation to manage security incidents, threats and vulnerabilities strategically. These documents will also assist the security head in preparing a projection of costs for a security budget. They may also serve as base documents to conduct performance assessments of personnel. The strategic objectives of this model are to reduce crime, increase detection rates and prevent losses. The model encourages the sharing of security information with all stakeholders and role players.

The organisation being protected should consider the role of security as important in protecting its assets and providing sustainability to its business activities. Security information should be seen as the lifeblood of any organisation. If the circulation of this lifeblood is cut, the organisation will not be able to sustain itself. It is important that the board of directors include security threats as part of their strategic plan. The organisation's board of directors should provide the organisational security strategy to address the identified threats. The organisational security strategy should indicate the prioritised threats, projected costs and time frames to address the specific threats. The security head should be a stakeholder on the board of directors, for the purpose of providing security advice and direction. The management of security information should be a permanent point on any board of directors' agenda.

The security head should manage security information in the three phases, namely collection of security information, analysis of security information, and the implementation of security risk control measures. A Security Information Management Centre (SIMC) should be established to equally manage the three phases. A Security Information Management Centre (SIMC) should handle the collection and the analysis of the security information. The SIMC should refer the analysis results with recommendations to top management in an analysis report. The analysis report should be handled by top management and referred, with recommendations, to the operational manager or the human resources manager for the implementation of management's decision.

The operational manager will need to project manage the implementation of security risk control measures within the context of strategies, physical protection systems, and actionable crime information products. The human resources manager will need to manage all workplace investigations. SIMC should manage all feedback reports on the implementation of management's decision. The security head responsible for all security-related matters in the organisation should develop a security plan to address the security threats using the organisational security strategic objectives as a directive. The security plan, which should consist of the threats affecting the organisation, information on vulnerabilities and incident-related information relevant to the threat, should be used to address the prioritised threats in terms of the allocated budget. In essence, the security plan will consist of a threat assessment document, a VA document and an IPA document. A qualified security analyst should prepare these assessment documents and it should be used as part of the security plan. The assessment documents should serve as tools to manage security risks, conduct performance management as well as impact studies on the PPS.

Collection of security information

A collection plan should be prepared to focus on the identified threat. The senior security officer should develop and manage this collection plan in accordance with project management principles. Collection capability should be intensified by making use of personnel, clients and security personnel from the organisation being protected. If feasible, organisations should consider establishing security information collection units. Responsibilities of security officials to collect security information pertaining to specific threats should be included in their contracts, job descriptions and service level agreements, whichever is applicable. Management should provide the required human, physical and financial resources for the collection of security information. Security officials should be trained in the collection of security information.

An awareness ethos should be created, so that personnel, clients and stakeholders become involved in the collection of security information. Security awareness procedures to encourage voluntary collection of security information should be advertised in the organisation that is being protected. Motivational programmes should be presented to personnel to intensify the collection of security information. Security personnel need to be skilled in the collection of security information. On the job training should be encouraged. The training curriculum should focus on the needs of the individual to perform the collection function. Psychologists/Criminologists should become involved in team building and life skills survival training to address the fear and victimisation that might occur during the collection of security information. There should be policies in place for the protection of witnesses against victimisation, so that people are protected against intimidation by criminals. The Witness Protection Programme should include an anonymous call number. Management should provide sufficient human, technical and physical resources to collect security information.

Policies are needed to guide the collection of security information in the security industry. Policy and standard operating procedures similar to that used by SAPS, SABRIC, PSI and the CGRI, should be designed for the collection of security information. The standard operating procedures should be inclusive of ethical standards to guide security personnel in the lawful collection of security information. In this way, all personnel will be aware of the collection cycle and the process to be followed. Security information protection measures should be put in place as a safeguard against information leaks and to overcome mistrust. Once the collector feels trusted, he should provide more information. This should enhance mutual relations. A cellphone system should be explored to enter all actionable information in SMS text and have it electronically relayed to the automated system in the security control room, SAPS crime control room and to the response team.

Workplace investigations should be made part of the private security provider's infrastructure as it will help in the collection of security information. The focus should be on collecting information by making use of informers, surveillance and undercover operations. Information collected during workplace investigations will enlighten management on the extent of unlawful activities and misconduct in their organisation.

The sharing of information should be encouraged by management. Sharing of information between management and grassroots personnel and with SAPS, NDPP and other security service providers with similar interests will go a long way in intensifying the collection of security information. External sources of information should be explored through networking and the signing of an MOU to access each other's databases. This will add value to the information on hand. Security service providers with similar interests should establish fusion centres so that joint sharing of information can take place. Security service providers should also participate in community policing structures and in the SAPS war room strategy established by SAPS provincial offices for the sharing of information.

Analysis of security information

All security service providers should create an analysis capability in their organisations. Security companies and the organisations being protected will need to establish analysis capabilities managed by trained and qualified security information analysts. It is important that qualified analysts should be employed to conduct security information analysis.

The organisational security strategy, the security plan and the needs of clients should be considered for the purpose of analysis. This is important to determine the projected costs allocated to address the specific threat confronting the organisation. This will help the analyst to prepare a recommendation based on the projected costs. Following this process will save the organisation human resources, technical and physical resources and money. Qualified analysts should be employed to conduct security information analyses according to the organisational security strategy and the organisational security plan.

The analyst should generate a threat assessment document, VA document and an IPA document. All security information collected on a daily basis should be used to populate these documents. These documents should serve as live documents, which will continue to inform the design and development of future collection plans. Security management should engage with analysts for the development of collection plans. The analysis of security information by qualified analysts will help in the identification of the correct vulnerability areas, so that the most appropriate operational responses may be provided to mitigate the risks. Personnel responsible for analysis should be given the necessary computer hardware and software resources to perform their tasks effectively. There should be adequate resources for the analysis of security information. There is a need for analytical computer software programs to assist analysts to generate innovative strategies and actionable information products. The organisational security strategy should indicate the type of hardware and software requirements to perform specific types of analyses.

Analysts should be given continuous training to keep them updated with technological advancements. All security service providers should establish data analysis capabilities. Line management should closely manage the analysis of security information function. Management should enjoy a relationship of trust with their analysts. Qualified analysts with operational experience should be utilised to design actionable information products, strategies, and recommendations for the PPS in consultation with the end users. Management should not interfere with the analysis function.

The reliability of the information source should be assessed on criteria such as the previous quality of information the source supplied, the situation, the location and likely access of the source at the time the information was collected. Data capturers or information managers should review all security information that is received. They are to ensure that the information is reliable, accurate and timely. The collected security information should be tested to determine if the collected information is sufficient for the analyst to conduct the relevant analysis.

There should be a collection capacity to assist the analysts to obtain missing information or any other information needed to enrich the information on hand. The completed document with all the relevant information should be sent to the analyst. Standard operating procedures should help in the data mining of all the collected security information. This should help to overcome the problem of information overload and to overburden analysts so that they do not achieve the organisational security strategy. The focus should be on threat and vulnerability information, as proactive action will prevent incidents from taking place. Methods used for the classification of information should be improved by enforcing a code of ethics among personnel and introducing information protection standards to control access where necessary. A standardised framework should be used for the analysis of security information. In this way, all personnel will be aware of the analysis cycle and the process to be followed.

Implementation of security risk control measures

The analysis report should be sent to management to make a decision on the implementation of the recommended security risk control measures. Security risk control measures should be implemented according to the organisational security strategy and the security plan. In this way, decisions will be made to give priority to specific threats that were not previously addressed or possibly not identified as such. Implementation of security risk control measures should be done in accordance with the allocated budget. Costs should not be an impediment to address the threat. Money spent on security risk control measures should be regarded as an investment and not a cost, because the purpose is to protect life and property, prevent losses and finally to also ensure business continuity. The aim, therefore, should be to reduce the threat with the available budget and not shelve the application of security risk control measures.

In making a decision on the implementation of specific security risk control measures, management must consider the security strategy, the security threats and the strategic objectives as identified in the organisational security strategy. In many instances security service providers use the reduction of crime, increase in detection rates and the prevention of losses as the strategic objectives to decide on the implementation of the most appropriate security risk control measures. Security risk control measures should be considered for implementation in conjunction with the organisational security strategy and the security plan. The security risk control measures should be directed at addressing specific threats, vulnerabilities and the recurrence of incidents according to the security plan.

The strategic objectives of the organisational security strategy should direct the implementation of the security risk control measures. Management should consider the design of the security risk control measures. The security risk control measures should be designed to address the strategic objectives. To design a specific security risk control measure, the security practitioner must take into consideration the organisation's operations and conditions to define the threat and identify the target. Security risk control measures need to be designed to deter, detect, delay and respond to intrusions. Organisations need to safeguard themselves against incorrect and illegally obtained information, which may be detrimental to the implementation of security risk control measures. Security personnel should immediately operationalise risk control measures relating to crime with the assistance of SAPS. The sharing of information on security risk control measures should take place at the Community Policing Forums and at special meetings held with SAPS. This will benefit the broader South African community by creating a much safer and secure environment. The challenge is for security managers to stay current on innovative design strategies. This knowledge should be coupled with the latest information on issues of changes in cultural values, crime, technology, market conditions and political conditions.

The approved implementation of security risk control measures should be disseminated in a formalised manner. It should preferably be a written communication. Experienced security personnel should be used for the implementation of security risk control measures. A project management approach should be used in the implementation of security risk control measures. Resources should be made available for the implementation of security risk control measures. The design of the security risk control measure should be quantitatively or qualitatively evaluated for deterrence of the adversary, detection of the adversary, delay of the adversary and response by security personnel. Some situations may require immediate action and prompt intervention. Some are cyclical, managerial and are amenable to technical solutions and problem-solving methods. Others are chronic, endemic difficulties that require the application of strategies over time, to change conditions and move an organisation ahead. There should be regular communication between the analyst and the end user. The end user should be allowed to request additional analysis of the security risk control measure. There should be a formalised manner in dealing with feedback from the end-user. It should preferably be a written communication. Line management should continually monitor and evaluate the implemented security risk control measure. A standardised framework should be used for the implementation of security risk control measures. In this way, all personnel will be aware of the implementation cycle and the process to be followed.

Government departments who employ contract security companies and those with in-house security services should have the security head as part of top management. The security head should be there to give strategic direction and guidance on security threats affecting the organisation, the organisational security strategy, strategic objectives and the security plan. Top management should make a commitment in terms of budget and resources to address the identified threats confronting the organisation. The procedures outlined above should be followed in the implementation of the SIMM. The security industry should consult with academic institutions responsible for providing academic qualifications in security management to offer a qualification in security information management, so that the qualification in security information management becomes compulsory for employment of security officials.

EXPOSITION OF THE MODEL

Issues related to specific security management need to be understood within a systematic context. Such an approach will provide a holistic, systematic understanding of the security environment, functions performed by security practitioners and insight of its body of knowledge. A systematic understanding of the security management related issues will avoid confusion and misunderstanding of the security organisation's existing functional processes. A discussion of the different management related issues will help understand the operational competency areas of a security environment.

The interpreted data as discussed in chapter 3 was used to design and develop a security information management model (SIMM). This model was discussed with specific security experts in South Africa and Australia (Australian Academic, 2011a–e; Australian Security Service Provider, 2011a, 2011c, 2011d; South African Academic, 2011; Conradie, 2010). They were strongly in favour of such a model to enhance security information management.

Figure 5.1: Security Information Management Model

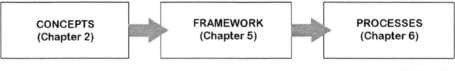

© D. GOVENDER

The model, which includes a framework, consists of three phases, namely the collection of security information phase; analysis of security information phase; and the implementation of security risk control measures phase. The collection and the analysis of the security information should be handled by the Security Information Management Centre (SIMC) and referred to top management as an analysis report (result/outcome). The analysis report is handled by top management and referred to the operational manager or the human resources manager with recommendations to design a treatment programme for implementation, feedback, monitoring and continual improvement of the security risk control measures. The SIMM (Figure 5.1) prepared by the author schematically presents the content of the Security Information Framework in Figures 5.2, 5.3 and 5.4.

Collection of security information

Figure 5.2: Collection of security information (Phase 1)

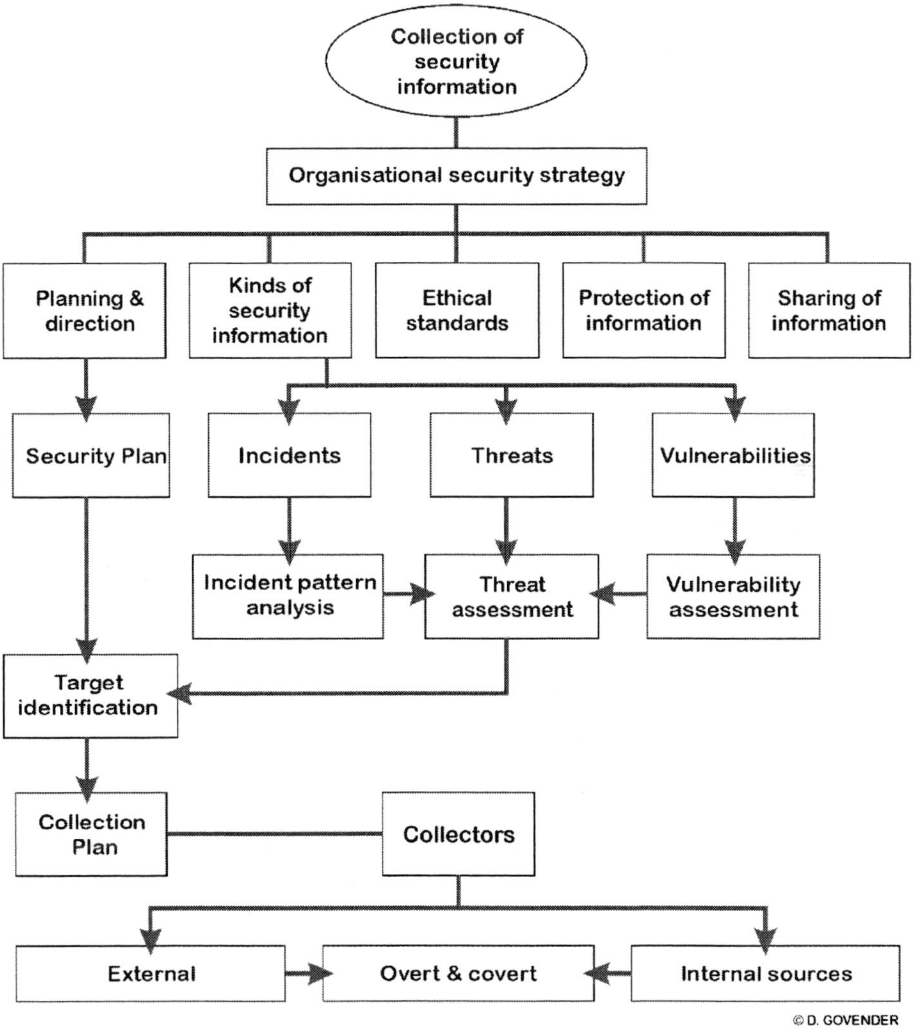

© D. GOVENDER

Organisational Security Strategy

The organisational security strategy for the collection of security information should provide for proper planning and direction at all levels of the organisation. It should provide for the different kinds of security information that should be collected and ensure that ethical standards are maintained and the sources are protected at all times. It should clearly indicate the different platforms where the security information might be shared and the manner in which the information may be shared.

73

Planning and/or direction

The **board** of directors and executive level management of the organisation being **protected** should develop a strategic plan. The strategic plan, among others, should **identify** the security threats affecting the organisation and its assets, as well as the **organisational** security strategy to address the threats. The threats should be identified **through** the process of a SWOT analysis conducted by the board of directors, executive **level** management and the security head. The organisation initiates a security survey **to identify** vulnerabilities relevant to the identified threats. An incident register should **be used to** identify incidents related to the threats. The incident register should consist **of reported** incidents experienced by the organisation (Jacobs, Shepherd, and Johnson, **1998).**

Planning is about collecting the right information that is needed to support top **management's** decision. It is about understanding the most important parts of the organisation, whether they are clients, government, technology, suppliers or competitors. The senior manager responsible for all security-related matters in the organisation, should develop a security plan to address the root causes of the security threats using the organisational security strategy as a directive. The organisational security strategy should indicate projected costs and time frames to address the root causes of the specific threats affecting the organisation and its assets. These threats will be prioritised in the organisational security strategy according to importance, taking into account the cost of losses if the specific threat has to occur. The security plan, which should consist of the threats affecting the organisation, information on vulnerabilities and incident-related information relevant to the threat, should be used to address the prioritised threats in terms of the allocated budget. In essence, the security plan will consist of a threat assessment document, a VA document and an IPA document. A qualified security analyst should prepare these assessment documents for use as part of the security plan. The assessment documents should serve as tools to manage the root causes of the threats, vulnerabilities and security risks, and to conduct performance management as well as impact studies on the PPS. A target-centred approach should be used to prioritise the threats for the collection of security information, analysis and implementation of security risk control measures (Clark, 2010).

Target-centred approach

The organisation should perform target identification. Targets may include critical assets or information, people, or critical areas and processes (Garcia, 2008). All stakeholders in an organisation, which includes senior management, collectors, analysts and operational management who are going to be involved in the collection and analysis of security information and the designing and implementation of the security risk control measures should be part of the target-centred approach. Here the goal is to construct a shared picture of the target, from which all stakeholders can determine what is expected of them to address the threat. They should be able to determine the resources they would need to do their jobs and what they can contribute from their own resources or knowledge to create a more accurate target picture (Clark, 2010).

Once a shared target has been identified, it is time to prepare a collection plan to focus on the threats and vulnerabilities affecting the shared target. The senior security officer should develop and manage this collection plan in accordance with project management principles. The collection plan should be developed in consultation with the security analyst. The security analyst should be able to provide guidance on the kinds of information to be collected and the key information needs in order to prepare specific analysis products in terms of the organisational security strategy.

Kinds of security information

Security information on incidents, threats and vulnerabilities should be lawfully collected in a structured manner within the ambit of an organisational policy framework. Standard operating procedures in line with the organisational policy framework should be developed to guide the collection of the different kinds of security information. The kinds of security information and the key information needs should be identified by the security analyst (Smit, 1989; Simonsen, 1998; Talbot and Jakeman, 2008). All personnel from the organisation, which is being protected, all security personnel, all stakeholders and clients of the organisation should be mandated to collect security information. Stakeholders and clients should be encouraged to provide security information, which they intend to voluntarily share with the organisation. Such security information may be regarding their own experiences, observation or on the activities of adversaries from the inside or outside of the organisation. Stakeholders and clients may be assisted by the mass media as to the types of security information required by the organisation. This may appear in pamphlets, posters, newspapers or on television screens as alerts, notices, etc.

A collection unit should be established within the Security Information Management Centre to collect security information and to assist the analysts in the collection of missing information. The Security Information Management Centre should manage all the collected information and provide rapid response to security information that requires immediate action. All the collected security information should be managed by the SIMC who should have the information evaluated/verified and entered into a computerised database. All security information should be collated by the analyst or a data capturer using an automated system with the relevant computer software. This should include indexing, sorting, and storage of raw information. A database should be created for storage. Only when similar information is collected and considered together can the analyst provide meaning to the information (Gottlieb et al., 1994).

The SIMC manager may task the collection unit to obtain missing information to ensure the data integrity of the collected security information. All threat information should be collated onto the threat assessment field, while vulnerabilities should be collated onto the VA field. The computerised system may be designed to also provide for an incident register to record all information on incidents. A computerised database will allow for the use of software to collate and analyse data into actionable information products (Talbot and Jakeman, 2008).

Collection process

The collection of security information should be mandated (authorised) by management either through job descriptions, service level agreements or through a code of conduct. Since the collection process is an act of gathering information on incidents, threats and vulnerabilities that may exploit the assets of an organisation and result in losses, management should give its full commitment to the security information management process (Fischer et al., 2008). Security information collection may also be outsourced to private security risk assessment companies (Fischer et al., 2008). The best sources of information are people and technology. All collected security information ought to be validated, as misinformation can result in bad decision-making. All employees in an organisation should be alerted to their responsibility of constantly reporting security information, which comes to their attention. The persons that should be approached first, from a tasking point of view, should be security personnel and those who work in the strategic areas as well as those that are well networked and attuned to the security information of the organisation (Muller, 2002c).

Personnel should be trained on how and what security information they should collect (Muller and Whitehead, 2002). Internal and external sources may be used to collect security information (Reuland, 1997). Ferraro and Spain (2006) identify methods such as physical surveillance, electronic surveillance, interviews, undercover operations, forensics, research and internal audit that can be used in collecting threat, vulnerability and incident information. The techniques that may be used to collect security information may typically include the overt information collection technique – which can be generally defined as personal interaction with people, and the covert information collection method, which is commonly defined as intelligence gathering (Lyman, 1988; Matthews, 1986).

Ethical standard

There should be a code of conduct signed by all personnel in service of the organisation that is being protected and by all security personnel. In the collection of security information, the collector must respect the law and the fundamental principles of privacy (Nemeth, 2010). Organisations and companies need their own set of ethical standards that should include issues such as preserving and protecting the organisation/company's credibility, value and public profile and what people may or may not do. Management should be clear about the fact that no unethical and illegal collection of information will be tolerated. When outsourcing certain aspects of security information collection, management should make sure that the contracted company knows the ethical guidelines in place in the contracting company or organisation. Transgressions by such contracted personnel will not exempt a company from liability, accountability and possible sanctions (Muller, 2002c).

Protection of information

The protection of security information is the prerogative of each organisation and should not be undermined in any way. The security protection measures applied by government departments are coordinated by a policy framework called the MISS. Private organisations, on the other hand, may structure their own standard operating procedures in line with their policy framework for the protection of security information. Security managers refer to the term "sensitive" when referring to information that has value and is protected. Organisations assign classifications to their "sensitive" information. The names assigned to the classification levels may vary from organisation to organisation and include secret, restricted, confidential, private and personal. Sometimes top secret and highly confidential is used, depending on the type of information being classified (Fay, 2006).

Personnel should be trained on how and what security information they should collect (Muller and Whitehead, 2002). Internal and external sources may be used to collect security information (Reuland, 1997). Ferraro and Spain (2006) identify methods such as physical surveillance, electronic surveillance, interviews, undercover operations, forensics, research and internal audit that can be used in collecting threat, vulnerability and incident information. The techniques that may be used to collect security information may typically include the overt information collection technique – which can be generally defined as personal interaction with people, and the covert information collection method, which is commonly defined as intelligence gathering (Lyman, 1988; Matthews, 1986).

Sharing of security information

The growth of information-sharing partnerships and networks and the recent development of "s" in the United States promise real-time information sharing and access for the future. Some security agencies uphold a "need-to-know" culture of information protection rather than promoting a "need to share" culture of integration (Ratcliff, 2009). Without a proper security information management culture and attitudes that favour the sharing of information, it is difficult to collect information in an organisation. Sharing of information goes hand in hand with the concept of having access to information databases under the control of other stakeholders and organisations. This includes working together with SAPS and other law enforcement agencies both nationally and internationally (Muller and Whitehead, 2002). There should be a plan for the sharing of information. Funding should be available for training, infrastructure, the development of standards, and the building of trust between law enforcement and the security service providers. The United States government identified not only the technological barriers to sharing information but also more importantly, the organisational and cultural barriers (Ratcliff, 2009).

Informal information-sharing networks are used when formal systems prove to be too tedious. This is not encouraged due to the leakage of information (Ratcliff, 2009). There are no punishments or sanctions for not sharing information (Ratcliff, 2009). According to Clark (2010), sharing requires openness. However, any organisation that requires secrecy to perform its duties will struggle with and often reject openness.

Analysis of security information

Organisational Security Strategy

The security analysis function includes evaluation and interpretation of security information. It should be directed by the organisational security strategy and the key security information needs that result from changes and action in the organisational environment. An event or development in the organisation could give rise to key information needs. The routine monitoring and evaluation of an effective analysis capability regularly uncovers information that has the potential to affect the strategy positively or negatively. The collected information should be properly organised to ensure that the right information is collected and gaps are determined. Organising the information means putting together relevant facts, developing appropriate titles and headings and then indexing the document for retrieval purposes. Factors such as chronology and geography can be used and information can be ordered according to appropriate themes. This is important for later retrieval and checking (Muller, 2002b).

An analysis function should be centralised because security information works on the principle of bringing together all relevant bits and pieces of data and information and adding meaning to it (Muller, 2002b). The analysis capability should be situated at the SIMC. The development of an effective analysis capability is really the true justification for establishing SIMC. If correctly focused information is not analysed and interpreted, the said information will be of little or no value to the end user. Understanding the organisation that is being protected can go a long way in easily accepting and influencing analysis results.

Figure 5.3: Analysis of security information (Phase 2)

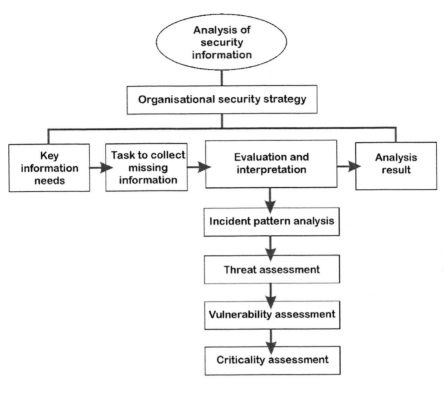

© D. GOVENDER

Three central points that analysts should recognise:

- decision-makers' internal environment exerts considerable pressure;
- decision-makers demand strategies and actionable information products over descriptive reports; and that
- growth from knowledge to strategy or actionable information products are dependent on the nature of the decision-maker (Ratcliff, 2009).

The standardised framework for the analysis of security information should provide for standard operating procedures. This should be approached in a multidisciplinary fashion. It should provide clarity on the following:

- what each person's input should be;
- deadlines;
- type of information required;
- most probable sources of information;

79

- **time** frame;

- **cost** estimate;

- **planning** for pitfalls, for instance, unavailability of information; and

- **framework** for final report themes, titles, format (Muller, 2002b).

Security information analysis is not a substitute for the analysis activities in areas such as sales, customer relations, the legal department, human resources, finance, market research, purchasing, or research and development. It would ideally add value through sharing and integrating of the information, and incorporating external information (Muller, 2002b).

Key information needs

The collected security information should be accessed from the computer by the analyst to confirm the key information needs in order to provide an analysis result in line with the organisational security strategy. Analysis of security information entails evaluation and interpretation of the exact nature of the problem and the characteristics of the incidents, threats and vulnerabilities. Important factors to consider include where the incidents are occurring, at what times, who is involved, how and why the problem is occurring, and what solutions have been tried in the past. By determining the underlying causes of the problem through the collection of detailed information, tactical strategies that are more effective can be developed to address the threats (Block, Dabdoub and Fregly, 1995).

Collecting missing information

Once the analyst has determined the key information needs and what information is missing or unavailable and where to find it, new tasking should be given to the collection unit or the responsible person for additional information. This new information will be used to enrich the information on hand, so that an accurate, complete analysis result may be produced (Muller, 2002b).

Evaluation and interpretation of information

The evaluation phase is the true analysis phase and has three aspects, that is, assessing, integrating and interpreting the information. The reliability of the information source is assessed on specific criteria such as the previous quality of information supplied by the source, the situation, the location, and likely access of the source at the time the information was collected. The accuracy of the information provided is assessed as an actual relative measurement in relation to each item of information received (Talbot and Jakeman, 2008). Although the reliability of the source needs to be assessed, the credibility of the information is also important and should not be neglected. The more primary information is used, the higher the importance of testing because of the subjective nature of human sources and the danger of mistaking misinformation and disinformation for fact. The information as well as where it was sourced, should also be tested for credibility and usability (Muller, 2002b).

According to Gottlieb et al. (1994), the interpretation of information is the true analysis function. It requires highly skilled and experienced security information analysts. These skills should include a variety of crime analysis tools, threat analysis tools, vulnerability analysis tools and criticality assessment tools. Incident pattern analysis will consist of incident patterns of both crime incidents and policy violation incidents. Since no literature could be found on IPA of policy violations in the security environment, the researcher decided on using the crime pattern analysis (CPA) process, employed by policing agencies. CPA contains information relative to continuing occurrence of particular criminal activities. They acquaint officers with the types of crimes being committed; list the days, times and locations of their occurrence; and provide officers with any known suspects, suspect vehicles, modus operandi, and/or property loss information.

Threats become more serious when vulnerabilities exist that can be exploited. There will always be potential threats in any protected environment. The threat should be assessed to ascertain the intent, capabilities and motive as this would affect the security risk control measures that would be devised and implemented. Therefore, being able to counter an actor's threat means knowing the actor's capabilities. For example:

- how effective is their intelligence capability?

- what measures would they employ?

- do they adhere to strict guidelines in terms of gathering information?

- do they have a history of using non-conventional methods, for instance, bugging? and;

- how determined are they or how desperate are they?

In identifying possible threat actors, one must not forget vendors, suppliers, customers, distributors, consultants and other indirect employees or associates. Do you really know them and their interests? What is it that they really know about the protected company's operations, plans, strategies, capabilities and weaknesses? How do they handle information of importance against the protected company? All organisations/ companies have areas of vulnerability and the bigger the vulnerability the more severe the threat. It is therefore important to assess the vulnerabilities. Potential vulnerabilities often include the following:

- a lack of defensive awareness among employees;

- unmaintained physical security protection systems;

- deliberate harmful actions by a disgruntled employee; or

- communication via telephones, facsimiles and even e-mail and the internet.

Information and other service vendors, consultants and service providers can also pose a threat. Weak links are usually people and the way they communicate with others. People's talkative habit may sometimes make them spill the beans. This step requires knowing the rivals' capabilities and expected actions. How would it go about "attacking" your vulnerabilities? Requirements for such an assessment are typically a record of dubious, often inexplicable incidents, for instance, stolen computers, break-ins and hacking incidents. Recognising vulnerabilities also means that companies are aware of potential loopholes and in time can take alternative measures to protect its interests. It is all about taking preventive measures to limit a potential threat (Muller, 2002a).

In criticality assessment the essential question is: How likely is it that a particular threat event will take place, or what is the probability of a threat event occurring? Has the product been a target before? What is the current situation regarding the threat? Was it previously attacked? If so, how frequently has it been attacked? The security manager must take into consideration the costs of replacement, repair, lost productivity, forfeiture of business opportunity, clean-up, litigation, damage to reputation and undermining of customer goodwill. Impact is always measured in rand value. Even when the impact is on human life, the yardstick is in rand value (Fischer et al., 2008: 157).

Analysis result

Analysing the information needed by clients can also pose problems, especially in terms of needs, the level of training of the analyst and the technical support in terms of the operating systems, hardware and software. The skills required may be considerably different from what they were initially employed for (Block et al., 1995).

"Relationship management" is not a term that many analysts are probably familiar with, but perhaps they should be. Managing the relationship between the analysts and the end user of the results, – the client – is essential if the knowledge possessed by the analyst is to be converted into actionable results. The need to manage this analyst–client relationship is the most vital skill that analysts should possess. "Relationship management" will help to overcome mistrust and misunderstanding between analyst, management and the end user (Ratcliffe, 2009).

Clarke and Eck (2003) are of the view that personnel appointed as analysts should be able to provide the kind of strategies, actionable information products and recommendations on PPS needed to support the end user.

There is a range of analytical techniques that can be used by analysts. Some of the analytical techniques include the following:

- Crime pattern analysis: provides trends and hot spot analysis.

- Network analysis: provides an understanding of the direction, frequency and strength of links between criminal collaborators in a criminal network.

- Market profiles: assessment of the market for a specific commodity, for instance, physical protection system.

- Demographic/social trend analysis: an assessment of the impact of socioeconomic and demographic changes on criminality.

- Criminal business profiles: determine and understand the business models and techniques used by organised crime groups.

- Target profile analysis: provides an understanding of the lifestyles, networks, criminal activities, and potential interdiction points in the life of a targeted offender.

- Operational intelligence assessment: evaluation of information collection to inform decision-making about an existing operation.

- Risk analysis: assesses the scale of risks or threats posed by offenders or organisations to individual potential victims, police and the public.

- Results analysis: a process used to evaluate the effectiveness of law enforcement activities (Ratcliffe, 2009).

Analysis report

Once the evaluation and interpretation have been completed and having determined how the analysis results should best be presented to management, the analysis results now need to be packaged. The analysis result should only consist of the answer to the original question and should not include comprehensive reports in which the answer is indiscernible. An effective analysis report should contain the following:

- a clear, concise and objective message that is responsive to the original key information need;

- be timely and in an appropriate format;

- contain varying predictions indicating most probable outcome;

- propose various proactive or counter-strategies;

- indicate information gaps and the effect thereof;

- comment on the credibility of information and reliability of sources; and

- use persuasive presentation skills (Muller, 2002b).

Implementation of security risk control measures

Figure 5.4: Implementation of security risk control measures (Phase 3)

© D. GOVENDER

Organisational security strategy

Upon receipt of the analysis report, top management may decide on the implementation thereof. They may use the analysis result to make recommendations to design appropriate security risk control measures that would deter, detect, delay and respond to an intruder or institute a disciplinary enquiry or civil/ criminal prosecution. Management may want to make personnel aware of specific activities. They may use it to deter or to authorise further collection of security information using physical surveillance or other unconventional methods. Ultimately, they may want to address the organisational security strategy by the implementation of security risk control measures in the form of strategies, physical protection systems (PPS), and actionable crime information products.

Objectives

No company can protect everything all the time. This would be unrealistic, impossible and unnecessary. We need to recognise that most organisations already have security measures in place, for instance, access control and firewalls. There is no need to double these efforts. Although there is limited linkage between an organisation's strategic plan and security functions, security risk control measures are often made the responsibility of security personnel. Once the vulnerable assets have been identified, those crucial elements in the assets should then be identified in order to design appropriate security risk control measures.

To formulate these objectives, the designer must understand the organisational operations and conditions, define the threat and identify the target. The ultimate objective of a security plan should be to reduce crime, increase detection and prevent losses. Typical objectives will be to prevent sabotage of critical equipment, theft of assets or information from within the facility, and protection of people. The envisaged security risk control measures must be able to accomplish its objectives by either deterrence or a combination of detection, delay, and response (Garcia, 2006).

Adversaries can be separated into three classes: outsiders, insiders and outsiders who are working in collusion with insiders. For each class of adversary, the full range of tactics (deceit, force, stealth, or any combination of these) should be considered. Deceit is the overriding of a security system by using fraudulent authorisation and identification; force is the overt, forcible attempt to overcome a security system; and stealth is any attempt to defeat the detection system and enter the facility covertly (Garcia, 2008).

Design

Using the objectives for security risk control measures obtained from the organisation characterisation, threat definition and target identification, the specialist can design security risk control measures. The security risk control measure design must be able to detect and detain (arrest) the adversary, prevent the criminal conduct or irregularity of the adversary from occurring and create awareness to prevent losses. In designing a specific physical protection system to avert the threat identified in the analyst's report, management must ensure that the new physical protection system will detect the adversary, delay the adversary, and alert the response force to interrupt the adversary.

Security risk control measures may be designed to include strategies encompassing crime prevention through environmental design (CPTED), business watch, car guard watch, neighbourhood watch, awareness, sharing of information, and electronic networking with other service providers and organisations. Many of these have served as best practices in the law enforcement environment. The challenge is for security managers to make themselves aware of current and innovative design strategies. This knowledge should be coupled with the latest information on issues of changes in cultural values, crime, technology, market conditions, and political conditions (Opolot, 1999).

Dissemination

Dissemination can be done in several different ways, namely, by attending briefings and strategy sessions, presenting verbal reports, providing written reports, having face-to-face contact whenever the need arises and public information systems – written and electronic media. To ensure that a paper trail exists, dissemination should take place in a regulated written format.

Implementation

The end user receives the recommended security risk control measure from management for implementation. The security risk control measure may take the form of strategies, PPS or actionable information products. There should be open communication between management, the analyst and the end user. This is important, especially where the end user needs to discuss a new trend or some additional design elements with the analyst or management regarding the specific threat.

Feedback

The last aspect after the implementation of the security risk control measure is feedback and reaction. Management and the analyst need to know what works and what does not work. Feedback may be given verbally or in written format. A survey form may be used to obtain feedback and reaction of the analysis result (Reuland, 1997).

Monitoring and evaluation

Once the security risk control measures have been implemented, they must be periodically reviewed to determine the effectiveness or lack thereof (Rogers, 2008). There are two main types of evaluations. They are outcomes and process evaluations. An outcome evaluation is to determine if the security risk control measure had the desired effect, such as, "was crime reduced?" or "was an intruder disrupted?" (Ratcliffe, 2009: 189). Line management should monitor and evaluate. It has to begin with a review and thorough understanding of the protection objectives the designed security risk control measure should meet. The PPS should be quantitatively and qualitatively monitored and evaluated for vulnerabilities on a continuous basis (Garcia, 2008).

CONCLUSION

This SIMM, developed using scientifically based information obtained during the implementation of the grounded theory design, puts forward concepts, framework and process. The justification for a SIMM is thus based on scientific data. The model aims to acquaint the security practitioner with the concepts relevant to security information management, which may be expanded by the practitioner according to organisational needs. The generic framework for the collection, analysis and implementation of security risk control measures will need commitment from top management in terms of strategic direction and funding. Chapter 6 will provide the security information process for the model.

CHAPTER 6

Security information management process

<table>
<tr><td>

OBJECTIVES

- Examine the diverse and interrelated disciplines of the South African Police Service and the private security industry in South Africa.

- Despite the efforts by the police, community programmes and private security, crime continues to be a major concern for most citizens in South Africa. Why?

- Understand the difference in meaning of sources, methods and techniques used to collect security information.

- Defend the recommendation that organisations should have their own security information analysis unit (SIAU).

</td></tr>
</table>

INTRODUCTION

Risk management has a long history, which started about 2 400 years ago in ancient Greece, where the Athenians always assessed risks before making decisions. The international standard ISO 31000:2009 serves as the theoretical foundation for risk management. This standard is currently being improved internationally by technical committees and working groups. Risk management developed in South Africa in the 1970s. Risk managers were also made responsible for finding innovative ways and procedures to reduce losses, which resulted in the integration of risk control and risk financing activities. The aftermath of the 11 September 2001 attacks on the World Trade Centre in New York and the Pentagon in Washington, D.C. identified many failures in security management. Some of the common failures include failure to formally collect security information on threats, vulnerabilities and incidents and have it analysed by qualified security analysts and to act on the information. Incidents, threats and vulnerabilities have the potential to affect an organisation's assets negatively. It is therefore necessary for this security information to be managed effectively and efficiently, so that correct decisions can be made on the implementation of security risk control measures. This chapter looks at the security information management process to reduce crime, increase detection rates and prevent losses.

ESTABLISHING THE CONTEXT

Context usually includes the internal and external organisational environments, organisational objectives and stakeholder identification. This context will determine the process to be followed. Despite the efforts by the police, community programmes and private security, crime continues to be a major concern for most citizens in South Africa (Van Rooyen, 2008). There is a close relationship between the rise of private security and changes to mainstream policing. Community expectations about the ability of the police to control and regulate crime have dropped and fear of crime has risen. Awareness has grown that paying for private security services is acceptable and sensible for individuals and corporations (Smith and Natalier, 2005).

According to Louw (2001: 4), the absence of an "information culture" in SAPS gave rise to problems in policing. The September 11, 2001, attacks on the World Trade Centre in New York and the Pentagon in Washington, D. C. have changed the face of security operations in South Africa and elsewhere in the world. A culture of security awareness about the importance of security information became a common theme considered by almost every person in the world (Fischer et al., 2008).

The value of security information in any organisation is the logical conclusion to a well-driven security awareness programme. Once people become aware of incidents, threats and vulnerabilities affecting the assets of an organisation, it is in their nature to react to it. Well-motivated people want to solve a problem if they feel concerned about it. A culture of security awareness is not an objective in itself; it is a state of mind and "the way things are done around the organisation" that support the achievement of broader organisational objectives. Establishing or even defining a security culture that will do this is not simple. Many attributes are involved to shape behaviours, attitudes and trust. Given the similarities between safety and security, we should consider the idea that a high performing security culture is also equally an informed culture (Talbot and Jakeman, 2008).

Security cultures are highly dependent on the knowledge gained from rare incidents, mistakes and near misses. Organisational culture, on the other hand plays a key role in incident reporting. The key element here is that the organisational culture has to support a no-blame environment where people feel safe to report near misses or minor events that might otherwise go unnoticed (Talbot and Jakeman, 2008).

Because of their positions in organisations and companies, security managers need to play a primary role in creating a thriving environment for the awareness of security information. According to Fischer et al. (2008: 149), "being aware of all possibilities is the characteristic of a good security manager. The best manager can think like a thief and thus is able to consider policies to reduce the vulnerability of company property. Therefore, a manager must develop the ability to analyse threats and vulnerabilities."

Managers are found in all areas of work and at different levels within an organisation ranging from supervisor to chief executive officer. They are responsible for running the organisation, developing strategies, setting targets and objectives, overseeing projects and coordinating activities. This is done to achieve performance targets and to ensure that everything runs smoothly. The size and scope of the responsibility may differ, depending on the size of the organisation, department, project, team or small business. There are certain common skills that managers need in order to manage security information effectively and efficiently. Managers need to:

- **plan** – decide how best to achieve the targets for a particular responsibility area;

- **organise** – decide on the most suitable ways of using resources (people, money, material and information) to maximise efficiency and profitability;

- **direct** – communicate effectively and guide others towards the organisational goals and objectives; and

- **control** – monitor and evaluate how the security plan is being carried out. This will involve setting timescales and target dates for goals and objectives and measuring progress at each stage. There may also be a need to adjust the plan to correct for delays and take advantage of new opportunities (Burt, 2004).

The collection of security information must follow specific legal procedures and processes. Information collection must involve all personnel and customers who are exposed to the organisation. It must cover the entire organisation. There should be proper management and control of the collected security information at all levels of the organisation. To put money into security information management is investing in the company's future (Fischer et al., 2008). Currently, very little notice is taken of threats, vulnerabilities and incident information on a day-to-day basis. If this information is collected immediately and acted upon, it will result in eliminating, disguising or minimising the vulnerabilities, so that threats do not materialise. The local environment may provide information about the threat for a specific organisation. Conditions outside the organisation and inside the organisation should be considered in this regard. Conditions outside the organisation, such as the general attitude of the community; whether the surrounding area is urban or rural; and the presence of well-known extremist groups, can provide information on threats. Conditions inside the organisation, such as the workforce, labour issues, industrial relations policies, security awareness and human reliability programmes, may also affect the potential threat (Smit, 1989).

An environmental scanning of the local and national population can be useful in determining a potential threat to a specific organisation. Any discontented and disgruntled group of the population should be addressed. Special attention should be given to war veterans, technically skilled people, political extremists and employees with experiences in or access to similar organisations. Several of an organisation's features may make it more attractive to an adversary if the adversary perceives such features as being to his/her advantage. A few of these features are the organisation's geographic and structural differences, the attractiveness of specific assets and the adversaries' assessment of vulnerabilities (Garcia, 2008).

There are two types of information on crime that are important, namely information as knowledge, which is provided first hand by victims, complainants, witnesses and offenders. This can be related directly to investigators and the courts. Information may also come from those who do not have first-hand knowledge of a crime, such as those from informants or opinions from experts. The second type is information as data, most often in the form of objects, documents, images, recordings and scientific samples from which investigators and courts can infer facts about the case (Stelfox, 2009).

Crime information must be timely, because the chances of apprehending an offender responsible for a series of cases depend on quick identification of the crime pattern (Goldsmith et al., 2000). Recorded crimes suffer from problems of under-reporting and are highly variable in their accuracy and quality, particularly in the way addresses and locations are geographically referenced (Hirschfield and Bowers, 2001). Even where crimes are reported and recorded by the police, the police record may contain a number of vague or inaccurate pieces of information. In some instances, the inaccuracies may be as a result of the interpretation put on the information by the recording official (Ainsworth, 2001). According to Gardner (2005), the quality of the processed information depends largely on how well a police service can store and access data. Reuland (1997) mentions that most organisations probably have few options for obtaining external information, since they have little control over external databases. According to Block et al. (1995: 3), the absence of a close working relationship with the community, incorporating an effective and mutual exchange of information, seems to be a problem in a community. The following problems were discovered in SAPS, pertaining to the collection of crime information at station level:

- the recording of exactly where crimes happened;

- the classification of certain crimes, for instance, aggravated versus common robbery, serious assault versus attempted murder; and

- updating the SAPS data sheet that provides information on the outcome of a case once it has been to court (i.e. whether a conviction was achieved, whether the case was withdrawn, etc.) (Louw, 2001).

In many instances, deductive or inductive arguments and rational reconstruction are not applied to collected information in the investigation of cases. Most detectives work in a routine and repetitive fashion, relying on knowledge information of complainants, victims, witnesses and suspected persons. The proper collection and analysis of crime information in the investigation of crime will increase detection rates (Altbeker, 1998).

Paulsen (2004) states that the field of policing has had an uneasy relationship with technology, often being slow to adopt new technologies despite their potential benefits to policing. Police agencies in the USA rely on the electronic transfer of data, laptop

91

computers transmitting data through radio frequencies or scan forms to ensure receipt of timely crime data (Goldsmith et al., 2000). According to Reuland (1997), although computers have had limitations in the past, an organisation needs to decide on the kind of technology that will be required for this purpose. The use of mainframe computers and microcomputers should be compared before making a choice. Mainframe computers are faster in their searching ability and can store far more data than their microcomputing counterparts. Mainframes are valuable, however, for storing and archiving data, as long as they can be easily accessed by microcomputers (smaller machines).

Collection of security information

The collection of security information on incidents, threats and vulnerabilities can be described as follows:

- incidents (crime/policy violations);
- threats (criminal, terrorism, foreign intelligence, commercial or industrial; competition and malice or other malevolent acts); and
- vulnerabilities (failures, non-application, under-application, erroneous application or superficial application of security risk control measures) (Smit 1989).

According to Talbot and Jakeman (2008), all incidents of crime and policy violations that take place in the organisation should be subject to investigation by the police or the organisation where the incident took place. An incident register should be used to record all reported incidents. The management of security incidents should be addressed in some detail in a policy document on incident management and reporting. The particular focus should be on the operationalisation of the information. According to De Kock (2011), all crime incidents in SAPS are recorded in registers and computer systems for analysis. This information is subsequently used to develop a CPA document for use by police officials in their day-to-day operations. He is of the view that the record of all incidents may also be used to develop an incident pattern analysis (IPA) document, similar to the CPA. Security officials may also use the IPA in their day-to-day operations.

Procedure on collecting information on threats begins with a strength, weakness, opportunity and threat (SWOT) analysis conducted by the organisation's top management. Management should prepare a security plan identifying the threats that have the potential to affect the organisation adversely. Management, in the preparation of the security plan, should also consider security information on incidents and vulnerabilities. The identified threats should be grouped according to their source, motivation and method of operation. This should be used to develop a threat assessment. The recorded incidents and the VA should be used to enrich the threat assessment. The threat assessment should be used to identify the targets to be addressed.

A collection plan should be developed based on the security plan for the collection of security information on the identified threats. The senior security manager should develop and manage this plan (Talbot and Jakeman, 2008).

Information on vulnerabilities may be collected during VAs, site survey/inspection or implicitly by observation and complaints received from clients or personnel. Information must be collected on any weakness or flaw in the physical layout of the organisation, procedures, management, administration, hardware or software that may be exploited to cause harm to the institution, business or activity (Simonsen, 1998). This information may be used to develop a VA document (Garcia, 2006).

Collection plan

The security manager should develop and manage a security information collection plan related to the threats. Security information on incidents and vulnerabilities must be taken into consideration in the preparation of the collection plan. The security manager must identify the threats that can become security risks for specific assets. The focus areas of the collection plan should be directed at the assets that are essential for the organisation to perform its function. It should be grouped according to the threat and consequent risk posed (Talbot and Jakeman, 2008).

According to Peterson (1994) and Bozza (1978), a systematic plan of action for the collection of information forms the basis of any security project. A collection plan shows what needs to be collected, how it is going to be collected and by what date. A collection plan may include a survey instrument, a chronological table and possible hypotheses that one intends to prove or disprove. A collection plan is usually approved by top management of the organisation being protected (Peterson, 1994).

Sources, methods and techniques used to collect security information

Sources

Sources for the collection of security information include intelligence sources, crime analysis documents, studies, professional organisations and services, published literature, government directives and legislation (Garcia, 2008). According to Smit (1989), vulnerability may give way to a security risk. Vulnerabilities can be typified as security weaknesses. Different types of vulnerabilities may present themselves where no or inadequate security risk control measures are in place. Examples of such vulnerabilities include unmaintained fences, rusted burglar bars, holes in fences, outdated alarm systems, poor supervision of personnel, insufficient security personnel on duty and vehicles not properly searched. Information on vulnerabilities also includes information on irregular and negligent acts. This information presents itself mostly as physical evidence. Security information may be collected on the following actions:

- failure to act (an omission)while in the employ of the company;

- **legal** duty was not carried out;
- **breach** of duty;
- **foreseeable** injury to other employees; and
- **actual** harm or injury to other employees (Fischer et al., 2008).

Information on the issue of crime may be described as "crime-specific elements that distinguish both one criminal incident from another and one group of offences, related in one or more ways, from a larger group of similar offences" (Reuland, 1997). Predefined crime data elements that may be collected include, for example the modus operandi such as points and methods of entry, the suspect's action, use of force or threats. It will also include information on a weapon and suspect's physical descriptors (Reuland, 1997). According to Van Heerden (1986), crime information entails solid or liquid material, which could establish an associative relationship between a person, weapon or vehicle and the crime or the victim. Crime information may present itself as either testimonial evidence or forensic evidence (Gardner, 2005). The collection of crime information is important, to assess the nature and distribution of crime efficiently, so that resources and personnel can be allocated. Workplace investigations are undertaken to establish whether an act, intention to act or omission may be labelled a crime or an irregularity. This creates an opportunity for management to get to know the activities taking place in an organisation. The information collected during the course of an investigation should be stored in the database and analysed with other information (Newburn et al., 2008).

Before collecting information in any investigation, the investigators should prepare themselves by obtaining all the relevant information that can assist them when interviewing witnesses. Information such as organisational charts, electronic files, personnel listings for potential interviews, financial statements, operational statements, public documents, press releases and internet postings may be used for this purpose, depending on the type of investigation being conducted. If there were anonymous tips, complaints or letters, this would be the time to obtain them as well (Van Rooyen, 2008). Corporate investigators are sometimes faced with intricate investigations such as white-collar crimes and protracted fraud investigations. They need to gather as much information as possible, from as many different sources as possible. In any investigation, information is the key to success and a start to the gathering of information must be made right from the beginning of the investigation (Montgomery and Majeski, 2005). According to Fischer (2004), investigating officers should have the ability to recognise, collect and use crime information in investigations. Crime information collected in the investigation of crime will assist the investigating officer to reconstruct the incident, ascertain the sequence of events, determine the mode of operation, uncover a motive, discover what property was stolen, find out all that the criminal may have done and recover physical evidence of the crime (Fischer, 2004).

External sources refer to databases under the control of other institutions and agencies. It is used to collect and store information that may be relevant to the decision-makers of another institution or agency. External sources can provide valuable information on adult career criminals and known offenders (Reuland, 1997). According to Block et al. (1995), "external data sources or data banks are often geographically based and information from parole and probation officers, mental health outpatient clinics, social services offices and similar agencies located in the most probable areas, can also prove to be of value. For example, a serial rapist in New York City emerged as a suspect after the investigator checked parolee records for sex offenders."

According to Reuland (1997: 9), "an inter-agency database was created in Jacksonville, United States of America, along with the juvenile courts, probation officers and social service agencies, to share offender-oriented information. In a short time, information about truancy, referral rates for absences, tardiness, behaviour problems, student conduct violations and academic history was made available for the purpose of creating a multi-agency supervision and intervention plan." A clear picture of disruptive incidents and trends emerged, along with additional knowledge of how youths interact with other students. From such an analysis, troubled youths could be identified faster and appropriate interventions applied more broadly. Such efforts were not possible previously, because the participating agencies had believed for a long time that information could not or should not be shared. The result was the maintenance of separate and usually incomplete files. Currently, most jurisdictions allow inter-agency sharing of juvenile information.

"The Chicago Police Department is supported by a geographic information system (GIS) called a geoarchive. Characteristics of the geoarchive are address-based data, information on both law enforcement and the community and an analysis that is used at community level" (Block et al., 1995: 222). The geoarchive acts as an institution-alised memory for law enforcement, holding not only law enforcement information, but also community information that is not always readily available to the local law enforcement official. The community data comes from a variety of city, state and federal agencies. "The law enforcement data and the community data can be used together for decision-making and problem-solving" (Block et al., 1995: 223–226).

Open source information from interviews with employees, neighbours, competitors, fire and ambulance crews, union representatives, security officers, postal employees, regular delivery drivers/suppliers and community members may serve as vital collection points (Broder, 2000).

Methods

Security service providers generally use a security survey instrument to conduct a security assessment of the organisation being protected. In addition to the information included on the security survey instrument, the security official is required to use observation and interviews to obtain pertinent information that may not have been required by the security survey instrument itself. Security surveys can take the form of a standardised checklist compiled at the discretion of management or a complex report. These assessments are carried out whenever the need arises (O'Block, 1981). A security survey is a critical on-site examination and analysis of an industrial plant, business, home, public private institution carried out in the light of a prevailing criminal threat. The security survey will determine the present security status, identify security deficiencies or excesses, determine the level of protection needed and make recommendations to improve overall security (Fennelly, 2004).

During workplace investigations, information is collected using different information collection methods. This task may be given to a corporate investigator in an organisation. A corporate investigator's function is highly skilled and challenging. A corporate investigator should have the knowledge and skills in information collection and fact-finding methods. It is the responsibility of the corporate investigator to select the most appropriate information collection method/s and use them properly to achieve the investigative objective (Smit, 1989). According to Ferraro and Spain (2006), although each information collection method may be used on its own, the best investigation results are usually achieved by combining them in some logical fashion. Some of the methods that can be used in collecting security information include physical surveillance, electronic surveillance, research and auditing, forensic analysis, undercover investigations, interviews and interrogation, physical surveillance, and various "techniques."

Physical surveillance

Physical surveillance takes place by either foot or vehicle, in order to follow a subject or subjects and this is called "mobile" or "tailing" or the investigator remains in a fixed position to observe a subject or subjects and this is called a "stakeout" or "static" surveillance (Ferraro and Spain, 2006).

Electronic surveillance

Electronic surveillance is similar to physical surveillance except that it is carried out with electronic technology, for example CCTV cameras (Van Rooyen, 2001).

Research and auditing

Research involves the examination of information from external sources, for example public records. Auditing applies to those records and documents internal to the organisation – specifically the examination of documents and information that would not normally be available to someone outside the organisation. These might include attendance records, productivity reports, personnel files, etc. (Ferraro and Spain, 2006).

Forensic analysis

Forensic analysis includes all forms of information gathering and analysis that employs science or scientific methods. Examples include bodily fluid analysis, chemical and substance analysis, fingerprint examination and comparison, accident, crime or incident reconstruction, computer forensics, various deception and detection methods (including polygraph) and forensic document examination (Ferraro and Spain, 2006). Ribaux et al. (2003), mention that there is considerable potential to combine forensic data with geographical information.

Undercover investigations

Undercover investigations, although complicated and difficult at times, can be of great value to the protection and preservation of corporate assets. However, undercover investigations should only be chosen as a measure when no other alternatives are available and when the company can reasonably expect a significant return on the investment. Therefore, knowing when and how to employ undercover investigations with the assistance of SAPS and the National Directorate of Public Prosecutions (NDPP) are critical for its success (Van Rooyen, 2008).

Interviews and interrogation

Van Rooyen (2008: 318–319), states that investigators experience the "information seeking interview" and the "admission seeking interview ." There are a few skills more important to the fact finder than the ability to obtain information through effective interviews and interrogation. Although volumes have been written on the subject, one needs to examine interviewing and interrogation as investigative tools to gather information in workplace investigations. The terms interviewing and interrogations mean different things to different people. Often these terms are used interchangeably, confusing both the user and the public. Many practitioners define interviewing as non-accusatory. This technique is used to gather information. Alternatively, the interrogation technique is seen as accusatory and its purpose is to gain the truth (Ferraro and Spain, 2006).

Techniques (means)

MacHovec (2006: 8), states that security officers also do electronic sweeps to detect "bugged" rooms, vehicles or equipment to prevent theft of trade secrets (for instance, a competitor's agent working undercover as an employee within the rival company/ business). They also protect executives from harassment, injury, kidnapping or terrorist attacks. As undercover employees or consultants, they can prevent fraud, theft, property damage or criminal acts by suppliers, employees or outsiders. Industrial security protects offices, factories, warehouses or prized possessions against damage or theft. Cybercrime investigators detect and prevent hackers from planting viruses or stealing credit card numbers or accessing a company's information and operational databases. The techniques or means used to collect crime information for the investigation of crime typically include the overt crime information collection technique, which can be generally defined as personal interaction with people and the covert crime information collection method. This is commonly known as intelligence gathering. The overt information collection technique is used to collect crime information through open means (Stelfox, 2009). Open means of crime information collection takes place by means of personal interaction with people and the perusal of public information sources. Many of the people who may provide open source information are complainants, witnesses to crimes, victims of crimes, suspects, journalists and representatives from agencies/institutions (Van Rooyen, 2008). Open means also include the collection of security information from television, radio, scientific journals, news bureaus, current affairs, grey literature, databases, images, maps, libraries, literature, academic public reports, private companies and people (Lyman, 1988). Scenes of crime may also be an open means for the collection of crime information as this is the location of observable information, which is gathered before it can be processed as evidence (Marais and Van Rooyen, 1990).

The covert crime information collection technique is used to collect crime information in a clandestine way or closed means. Closed means of collecting crime information refers to actions of people who are generally known as informants or agent provocateurs. These informants or agent provocateurs carry out clandestine operations to obtain crime information for the investigation of crime (Matthews, 1986). According to Lyman (1988), closed means include the use of physical surveillance, electronic surveillance, informants and undercover officers, for purposes of reducing crime, increasing detection rates and preventing losses.

According to Altbeker (1998), in order to move against the leader of a criminal group or syndicate, it is necessary to have information and evidence. Information can be obtained through closed means, namely electronic interception of communication from informers and agents. If recordings of conversations or intercepted mail are to be used as evidence, permission must be obtained for these procedures and information supplied by an informer or agent can only be used in court if the person is prepared to testify. For that reason, the police tend to use agents, because, as paid police officials, they are certain to testify. Informers, on the other hand, who are associates of the subjects, usually refuse to testify or may be discredited when they do. Police officers can provide valuable advice on the application of covert information techniques (Stelfox, 2009).

Despite the potential for the use of closed means, there are resource constraints when using these means, as they are costly, require high levels of commitment and skill and most importantly, require visionary and innovative managers. Confidential sources need to be employed in a more proactive, strategic and targeted way, so that the benefits can outweigh the risks (Ratcliffe, 2009). For these reasons, closed means are mainly used to guide investigations into syndicate crime. The difficulty, however, is ensuring that the information gathered can eventually be used as evidence in court (Altbeker, 1998).

Security information collection capacity

The National Strategic Intelligence Act, No 39 of 1994 was legislated to carry out the functions as stipulated in section 210 of the Constitution of the Republic of South Africa Act, No. 108 of 1996 (South Africa, 1994; South Africa 1996). This national legislation empowers specific government agencies to maintain an intelligence collection capacity, for the sake of national security. SAPS have a crime intelligence gathering unit that gathers intelligence for the purpose of policing (De Kock, 2011). The private security industry is excluded from this legislation. The Private Security Industry Regulatory Act, No. 56 of 2001 does not provide for the management of security information in the security industry in South Africa (South Africa, 2001).

Security information management in the South African security industry is not given the same attention as risk management internationally. Emphasis is placed on identifying vulnerabilities, studying of risks and optimising risk management alternatives. Human resources and technology are seldom used to obtain information on incidents, threats and vulnerabilities. According to Garcia (2008), to understand an organisation, information on many different aspects of the organisation must be obtained and reviewed. This includes obtaining information on the threat definition as well as the target that needs to be protected. The required information needs to be defined by management and organised to make it usable. The information of adversaries may include information on motivation, potential goals based on targets, tactics, numbers and capabilities. Sources of information should include intelligence, crime studies, professional organisations, published literature, policy, legislation and many more (Garcia, 2008).

In the United States of America, the collection of security information in the private security industry is authorised by management. The information is directed at safeguarding an organisation's assets against threats. Information is collected on incidents, threats and vulnerabilities that may exploit the assets of an organisation and result in losses (Fischer et al., 2008). Many security service providers use investigators to collect security information. Investigators need to master the art of information collection. Information is everywhere; investigators need to know what to look for and whom to ask. It is therefore important to encourage workplace investigations in order to maintain such a collection capacity (Nemeth, 2010). Security officers only collect security information when conducting investigation on incidents for the sake of disciplinary investigations or reporting to the police.

Information collected on a daily basis is very seldom analysed or enriched as intelligence for implementation. This is because many security service providers do not have an intelligence analysis capability. This information is handled by supervisors and given to the police where necessary. According to Jordaan (2003b), timely and actionable security information must be enriched into intelligence or evidence by the intelligence unit/collection unit or the investigator, who may add value to the collected information.

Companies also engage private investigators to collect information for them. Some security companies also have their own security information collection capacity. Common businesses and industries create central repositories of security information deemed important to their common interest nationwide and make it available in various ways to their separate groups (Fischer et al., 2008).

Sharing of security information

Information-sharing is the act of exchanging information between collectors, analysts and end users to help them function more effectively and efficiently. In South Africa the need to share security information with SAPS is a necessity to ensure a reduction in crime rates and an increase in detection rates. Simultaneously, users need to protect the information made available to them. The inability or unwillingness to share this information was recognised as a weakness by the office of the Minister of Safety and Security (South Africa). The Minister called for "partnership policing" between the police and private security service providers to enhance the sharing of information. This call, which proved to be excellent in facilitating greater sharing of information, is a start to shaping policy and governance around information-sharing between the private security industry and SAPS. The abovementioned statement by the Minister of Safety and Security was endorsed in 2011, by the Minister of Police when it was acknowledged that private security companies contributed in reducing crime for 2010/2011.

Clark (2010: 54–55) states that: "Fusion centres and war rooms were originally started to share information in support of homeland security in the United States of America (USA). The short-fuse synthesis (often called fusion) differs from normal synthesis and analysis only in the emphasis that "time is of the essence." Fusion is aimed at using all the data sources to develop a more complete picture of a complex event, usually with a short deadline. The analyst is there to fit in any new or additional incoming data as well as anything that is immediately accessible to them in a database or in memory." The security information management companies in South Africa use the fusion centre approach to handle current incident-based information, to support ongoing operations and to allow additional collection to be done in a shorter period. The need for this type of information has domestically led to the creation of fusion centres to support their clients, beneficiaries, SAPS and other stakeholders. These fusion centres integrate information coming from business, private security providers and SAPS (SABRIC, 2010). SAPS also have fusion centres, which have been created along the lines of war rooms. The SAPS War Rooms handle diverse sources and types of information on threats. These war rooms exist provincially in SAPS. Some of the so-called war rooms have done very little fusion work with the private sector (De Kock, 2011).

The Private Security Industry Regulation Act, No. 56 of 2001 of South Africa, provides for the promotion of a legitimate private security industry. It acts in terms of the principles contained in the Constitution and other applicable laws. It directs the industry to act in the public and national interest in rendering security services. Section 5 of the Act, read with Section 6, provides for the governance of the private security industry (PSI) by the Private Security Industry Regulatory Authority (South Africa, 2001). The Private Security Industry in South Africa has played a supportive role in helping SAPS to combat crime for many years. As a fast-growing industry, the question that comes to mind: "Is the private security industry doing enough to support SAPS in the sharing of information of an operational and strategic value?" If not, what are the challenges and what should be done to overcome these challenges? Private security service providers should collect security information on threats and vulnerabilities on a daily basis. It should be shared as raw information, products, strategies and/or actionable information products on an informal or formal basis with SAPS. It will assist them in the prevention and control of crime. According to Minnaar and Ngoveni (2004), to promote partnership policing it is felt that not only the raw information should be shared but that the collection, analysis and dissemination of information should be managed on a formal and organised basis (specifically by means of an Information Protocol).

Ethics in the collection of security information

In the collection of security information, the gatherer must respect the law and the fundamental principles of privacy (Nemeth, 2010). Information must always be collected in accordance with the Constitution of the Republic of South Africa, Act, No. 108 of 1996 and any legislation that regulates the obtaining of such information. Whenever it becomes necessary to use an information collection method, the investigator should consult with the legal adviser of the corporate for legal advice (South Africa, 1996). In the South African context, information and facts should be collected in accordance with the following legislative requirements:

- National Strategic Intelligence Act, No. 39 of 1994

- Protection of Information Act, No. 84 of 1982

- Protection of Personal Information Act, No. 4 of 2013

- Promotion of Access to Information Act, No. 2 of 2000

- Protected Disclosures Act, No. 26 of 2000 (the so-called Whistle-blowers Act)

- The Constitution, Act, No. 108 of 1996

- Interception and Monitoring Act, No. 127 of 1992

- Section 252A of the Criminal Procedure Act, No. 51 of 1977 (South Africa 1977; South Africa 1982; South Africa 1992; South Africa,1994; South Africa 1996; South Africa 2000a; South Africa 2000b; South Africa 2013)

There have been a few visible problems with the misuse of information in South Africa. This led to strong public and media criticism (De Kock, 2011). In hindsight, it is apparent that most of these problems were the result of poor management of security information.

Du Preez (1996: 16–17), states that: "the continued possession of information, from the time it is first collected until it is presented in court as evidence, must be assured – as well as its control, coordination and cumulative use." It is important to ensure the integrity of information collected. This will avoid legal restrictions that may prevent the introduction of such information as evidence at a trial or the development of a solid case for prosecution (Gardner, 2005: vii).

The collection of information for the investigation of crime must be conducted in a lawful way, so that the evidence being presented will indeed be admissible as evidence. The evidence must also be of such a nature that the unlawful act of the accused is demonstrated beyond any reasonable doubt. For this reason, systematic and planned action is an essential part of criminal investigation (Van Heerden, 1986).

Analysis of security information

There are four types of analysis, which are often used by law enforcement in combating crime. They include crime analysis, intelligence analysis, operational analysis and investigative analysis. These types of analyses may also prove to be useful to security practitioners for reducing crime, increasing detection rates and preventing losses (Gottlieb et al., 1994). Traditionally, much of the analysis was carried out mentally by seasoned managers who used to pass down techniques to colleagues by word of mouth. The advent of the modern computer, however, has allowed the police and other agencies to have more sophisticated systems to help understand crime patterns (Ainsworth, 2001). Analysis can be done manually or through computer systems, though many agencies prefer the automated approach. Reuland (1997) is of the opinion that expensive computer applications are not the answer, as they are no substitute for analytical creativity. The analyst's skill, experience and creativity usually determine what to look for and computers only expedite the process.

Manual processing of actionable crime information products can be traced back to the early 1900s, when August Vollmer introduced the English technique of systematic classification of known offender modus operandi (MO). Manual analysis entails the systematic manual analysis of daily reports of serious incidents. This is done to determine the location, time, special characteristics and similarities to other similar incidents. It can also help with various significant facts that may help to identify either a criminal or the existence of a pattern of criminal activity (Block et al., 1995). The change from manual analysis to automated analysis is important, not only because it supplements the expertise of experienced officials, but also because the knowledge and techniques accumulated over the years do not retire with the official. It is there for others to build on (Block et al., 1995). Crime mapping and geographical profiling (which is done manually on a map by using a selection of different-coloured pins, each of which represents a crime or incident that has taken place) are useful in showing crime hot spots and allowing decision-makers to see at a glance where crime is concentrated. Such information assists managers to allocate their resources more effectively and to focus their policing on those areas that appear to have the highest crime rates (Ainsworth, 2001).

One of the most important purposes of crime information analysis in the investigation of crime is to identify and generate crime information products needed to assist in the investigation of crime (Goldsmith et al., 2000). An analyst is responsible for turning the raw security information into timely and actionable crime information products, which can be used by an investigator for crime investigation. The timely and actionable crime information product is enriched into court-directed evidence by the investigator, who adds value to the crime information product (Atkin, 2000). During the analysis stage, staying objective and keeping a broad perspective is crucial to success (Clark, 2010). Clarke and Eck (2003) are of the view that personnel appointed as analysts should be accustomed to providing the kind of analysis results needed to support the end user. This means that analysts should:

- know how to use modern computing facilities and how to access and manipulate comprehensive databases;
- know how to use software to map incidents, to identify hot spots and to relate these to demographic and other data;
- be able to routinely produce actionable crime information products such as charts showing weekly or monthly changes in crime at force and beat level, perhaps to support compstat-style operations;
- be accustomed to carry out small investigations into such topics as the relationship between the addresses of known offenders and local outbreaks of car theft and burglary;
- carry out some before and after evaluations of crackdowns, say, on residential burglaries or car thefts;
- have some basic knowledge of statistics and research methodology such as that provided by an undergraduate social science degree; and
- be able to recommend security risk control measures for consideration by management.

Analysts must think of themselves as experts; they must know what works in the investigation of crime; promote problem-solving; learn about environmental criminology; develop research skills and communicate effectively (Clarke and Eck, 2003). Individual analysts should be appointed to service a team of investigators specialising in specific investigations, so that there is continuous collection, analysis and recommendations on security risk control measures (Goldsmith et al., 2000).

It is evident from Reuland (1997), and Redpath (2004), that an organisation working with security information should have its own security information analysis unit (SIAU) with appointed analysts functioning under the control of a manager. An SIAU ought to be seen as a sub-component of security information management. Hirschfield and Bowers (2001), support the use of automated systems. According to them, with a little effort and very little analysis expertise, it is possible for an analyst to produce actionable information products by following directions on the computer system.

Most departments have at least three choices. One option is to develop an in-house analysis system. Another option is to contract with an independent vendor who would custom-design a system for the organisation. The third option is a system transfer. With this last option, the agency obtains a portion of a computer software application that was developed for or by another agency. The extent of the transferred information can occur at one of three levels, namely concept transfers, design transfers and operational transfers (Reuland, 1997).

As microcomputers become the preferred analysis platform, system transfers from more advanced departments to less advanced ones will undoubtedly become more prevalent. The advantages of the transfer option include the specificity of these programs to security information and the low cost associated with working directly with another security service provider (Reuland, 1997). According to Block et al. (1995), because microcomputers have become more affordable and powerful, computer applications have become a practical tool in analysis. Analysing the information needed by investigating officers can also pose problems, especially in terms of the investigating officers' needs, the level of training of the analyst and the technical support in terms of the operating systems, hardware and software (Block et al., 1995). The final impact of the analysis lies in the monitoring and evaluation of the application of the security risk control measures. One of the most important responses developed to overcome obstacles has been the effort to create systems of information management, as well as methods of prioritising potential suspects so that investigations can proceed in the most effective and efficient manner possible (Block et al., 1995; Peterson (1994).

Evaluation/Verification

All security information collected from different sources must be evaluated/verified before undergoing any form of analysis. This will avoid unnecessary costs, time and energy. According to Talbot and Jakeman (2008: 142), "the Admiralty Scale is commonly used as a technique to quality control security information received from sources. The scale provides a means of rating the reliability and accuracy of collected information through a graduated alphanumeric scale, hence determining the usefulness of the information." The reliability of the information source is assessed on criteria such as the previous quality of information provided by the source, the situation, the location and likely access of the source at the time the information was collected. Each item of information received is assessed for accuracy before the collected information is analysed for application.

Collation

The analyst or a data capturer using an automated system with the relevant computer software collates all evaluated /verified security information. Collation is defined as the indexing, sorting and storage of raw information (Reuland, 1997). Raw information in itself is seldom of much value. Only when similar information is collected and considered together can the analyst provide meaning to the information (Gottlieb et al., 1994). Effective collation of threat information requires communication with the client that originated the threat and the interpretation of the information requirements. A limitation of many existing police collation strategies is the dominance of only the internal source of information. Over-reliance on just the internal law enforcement information sources places considerable limitations on the quality of the information (Ratcliffe, 2009). To improve the quality of the information, analysts will have to enhance the collation mechanisms with information from external organisations and this brings us back to sharing of information. Information collation is therefore seen as a challenge to modern policing. This includes improving of information sharing, the question of whether liaison officers can resolve information-sharing problems and the role of information from confidential informants in strategic decision-making (Ratcliff, 2009).

Incident Pattern Analysis

Incident pattern analysis (IPA) in the security industry will consist of incident patterns of both crime incidents and policy violation incidents. Since no literature could be found on IPA of policy violations in the security environment, the researcher decided on using the crime pattern analysis (CPA) process employed by police agencies. According to Gottlieb et al. (1994), CPA contains information relative to continuing occurrence of particular criminal activities. This CPA acquaints officers with the types of crimes being committed; lists the days, times and locations of their occurrence; and provides officers with any known suspects, suspect vehicles, modus operandi and/or property loss information. Information concerning the preferred target of attack (victim and/or property) should also be included, as should results of past analyses or predictions as to when and where suspects may strike again. Alerts should be updated until suspects are arrested or the pattern ends. These crime patterns are used by officers on patrol to create directed patrols or tactical action plans. Patrol officers are given as much information as possible to enable them to develop a strategy, which effectively deals with a problem (Reuland, 1997). This is accomplished by providing patrol officers with a narrative description of the incidents, a map depicting past and future locations of occurrence and any graphs that clarify the problem (Paulsen, 2004).

The geographic identification of patterns of crime means that certain types of similar crimes occur frequently at particular spots. By applying the geographic identification system (GIS), a CPA document can be retrieved from the GIS for application by end users (Horne, 2009).

Threat assessment

Once the security information on the threats has been identified, the key is to consider the specific threats in a given situation. Each individual organisation will have unique threats. Therefore, individual managers must develop the ability to do threat assessments (TAs). A thorough threat assessment, if comprehensive and accurate, will lead to the implementation of effective security risk control measures (Fischer et al., 2008). Threat is usually assessed and described using a combination of intent and the capability of a threat actor, whether individual or organisational, to attack or adversely affect an organisation or its assets (Talbot and Jakeman, 2008). Threats may vary from one organisation to another. In addition, one organisation may face several different threats compared to another. This will depend on the nature of the organisation and the operations being conducted by the organisation. Threats are usually directed at specific targets. A threat also includes anything that has the potential to prevent and hinder the achievement of objectives or disrupt the processes that support them (Garcia, 2008). The first activity in any security information management process is to understand the threat. It has to be determined beyond all reasonable doubt if the threat exists and the risks posed by the threat to the organisation and its assets. If the threat poses a risk, the targets for attack must be determined, so that security risk control measures can be applied.

People, mechanical failures or management systems can create threats. People are not only capable of deliberate actions to release hazards or cause loss, but also have the capability of applying creative intellect to their misdeeds (Fischer et al., 2008). The ability to apply intelligence enables human beings to identify and evaluate any existing security barriers and to devise and test ways of bypassing them.

During the analysis of security information, the threat is discussed with subject matter experts and intelligence officers. Analysts should review past incidents related to the threat. Open source information is also collected on the threat. Such an approach almost invariably involves some element of subjective estimation. In such situations, one way of determining the likelihood of threat occurrence is to rely on the knowledge and experiences of subject matter experts and information/intelligence collection units. All attempts to fill in the information holes should be based on their considered contributions. Once a threat assessment has been completed, typical processes related to the application of security risk control measures would commence. To identify the security risks posed by the threats, there are three specific methods that may be used to do the threat analysis. Threat analysis is an organisational security risk analysis process. Security risk professionals who are informed by generic risk analysis information (Talbot and Jakeman, 2008) conduct a threat analysis. In the *first method*, the analyst must determine if the source has the potential, motive and operational capability to carry out the threat. In the *second method*, the analyst should focus on the assets (functions, resources and values) that are essential for the organisation to perform its role and group them according to the threat and consequent risk posed. In the *third method*, the analyst should look at the organisational exposures or vulnerabilities and then use them to review the suitability of existing security controls.

Vulnerability assessment

physical protection systems (PPS) include all security products and technology. The primary functions of these PPS are detection, delay and response. Both quantitative and qualitative methods of vulnerability assessment (VA) may be conducted on PPS. It is very important to determine before the start of the assessment whether a quantitative or qualitative assessment method will be used. Quantitative assessments are recommended for facilities with huge asset losses. Qualitative assessment can be used if the asset values are much lower. When performing VA, the general purpose is to evaluate each component of the PPS to estimate their performance as installed at the organisation. Once this is done, an estimate of the overall system performance is made. The key to a good VA is accurately estimating component performance. When using a quantitative approach, this is done by starting with a tested performance value for a particular PPS component, such as a sensor and degrading its performance based on how the device is installed, maintained, tested and integrated into the overall PPS. For qualitative analysis, performance of each component is degraded based on the same conditions, but the performance of the device is assigned a level of effectiveness, such as high, medium or low rather than a number. In addition, component performance must be evaluated taking into consideration the weather conditions, the existing condition of the organisation and all the threats affecting the organisation (Garcia, 2006).

When VA is dealt with as part of the security management cycle, it should be a continuous process. A VA is carried out by collecting information on the PPS. The specific PPS is checked to ascertain if it can detect an intrusion, generate an alarm and then transmit that alarm to a location for assessment and response. The organisation is reviewed to determine if it conformed to all legal and administrative compliance requirements. A checklist is used to document the presence or absence of components and component parts. A deficiency report is prepared with notes if the component is not compliant. The VA report summarises these findings and the organisation makes improvements according to its organisational policy (Garcia, 2006).

Criticality assessment

According to Talbot and Jakeman (2008), criticality assessment is a vital step in the identification of risks. It assists in the prioritisation of threats and understanding of an organisation's vulnerability to those threats. It also assists with risk identification as well as analysis and the application of security risk control measures in order to focus on priority assets that are of utmost importance to an organisation. Criticality assessment determines the probability of loss due to an incident, threat or vulnerability and the impact the loss will have on the organisation.

Probability

Once security information on incidents, threats and vulnerabilities have been collected and analysed, it is essential to determine the probability of loss. When security managers are confronted with a series of problems, they must determine which problems need immediate attention. According to Le Roux (2004) and Fischer et al. (2008), probability is a mathematical statement concerning the possibility of an event occurring. Unfortunately, such mathematical precision must wait until various subjective security measures can be turned into numerical values. The best we can do today is to make subjective decisions about probability. Such decisions should be based on data such as the physical aspects of the incidents, threats and vulnerabilities being studied, for example criminal acts, spatial relationships, location and composition of the structure. Procedural considerations must be studied together with the policies of the organisation. The history associated with the industry is of great importance, particularly the incident, threat or vulnerability being studied. The essential question is, How likely is it that a particular threat event will take place? Has the product been a target before? What is the current situation regarding the threat?

Impact

To separate the security information on incidents, threats and vulnerabilities into finer categories, security managers use the principle of criticality. The term has been defined as the impact of a loss in rand (South African currency of money). The impact of the threat is an approximation based on the organisation's prior experiences and the experiences of similar companies in similar situations. The rand is the customary measure of impact. The security manager must take into consideration the costs of replacement, repair, lost productivity, forfeiture of business opportunity, clean-up, litigation, damage to reputation and undermining of customer goodwill. Even when the impact is upon human life, the yardstick is a rand value. The impact is also determined by the following:

1. Replacement cost (other indirect costs);

2. Temporary replacement (hiring costs);

3. Downtime (business is not as usual);

4. Discounted cash (withdrawals from investment);

5. Insurance rate changes (increase in premiums); and

6. Loss of marketplace advantage (product cannot be delivered on time) (Fischer et al., 2008).

Impact is an extremely important concept for security managers to understand. In general, company managers who usually think in terms of cost/benefit analysis, will not be interested in spending money for security if the cost is greater than the potential loss of money. Impact, much like probability, is a subjective measure, but it can be placed on a continuum. It is possible to quantify security risks somewhat and to determine which risks merit immediate attention by using the rankings generated for probability and impact and devising a matrix system for various security risks. Using the matrix, probability and impact alphanumerical values can be assigned to each security risk. If a choice has to be made, impact should take precedence over probability (Fischer et al., 2008).

Implementation of security risk control measures

The analysis of the collected security information will identify specific risks that will need security risk control measures. These risks will require the implementation of specific security risk control measures. The security risk control measures may take the form of physical protection systems (PPS), strategies and actionable crime information products. Management should determine the protection objectives for the implementation of the security risk control measures. Examples of protection objectives may include abilities to detect and arrest the adversary, reduction of crimes or irregularities or the prevention of losses (Garcia, 2008). Given the protection objectives, the designer should be able to design the most appropriate physical protection system, strategy or actionable crime information product. The designed security risk control measure with recommendations is disseminated to line managers for implementation, monitoring, evaluation and feedback.

Determine objectives for security risk control measures

The first step in the process is to determine the objectives for security risk control measures. To formulate these objectives, the designer must understand the organisation's operations and conditions, define the threat and identify the target.

A thorough description of the organisation and the processes within the organisation is required. This information can be obtained from different sources, including the organisational design blueprints, process descriptions, safety analysis reports and environmental impact statements. A tour of the organisation and interviews with the personnel are necessary. This will provide an understanding of the physical protection requirements for the organisation as well as an appreciation for the operational and safety constraints. Additional consideration will also include an understanding of liability and any legal regulatory requirements, which must be followed. Each organisation is unique, so this process should be followed each time a need is identified.

In defining the threat, specific information needs to be considered. If this information has not yet been collected, additional tasking needs to be given for the collection of this information. The additional information needs to answer three questions about the adversary:

1. What class of adversary should be considered?

2. What is the range of the adversary's tactics?

3. What are the adversaries' capabilities? (Garcia, 2008).

Adversaries can be separated into three classes: outsiders, insiders and outsiders working in collusion with insiders. For each class of adversary, the full range of tactics (deceit, force, stealth or any combination of these) should be considered. Deceit is the attempted defeat of a security system by using false authorisation and identification; force is the overt, forcible attempt to overcome a security system; and stealth is any attempt to defeat the detection system and enter the facility covertly. For any given facility, there may be several threats, such as a criminal outsider, a disgruntled employee, competitors or a combination of the above. The PPS must be designed to protect against all these threats. Choosing the most likely threat, designing the system to meet this threat and then testing to verify the system's performance against the other threats will facilitate the process. Finally, target identification should be performed for the organisation. Targets may include critical assets or information, people or critical areas and processes. A thorough review of the organisation and its assets should be conducted. Such questions as "What losses will be incurred in the event of sabotage of this equipment?" will help identify the assets or equipment that are most vulnerable or that create an unacceptable consequence (Garcia, 2008).

Design security risk control measures

Given the description of the organisation, threat definition and target identification, the designer can determine the objectives of the security risk control measures. Examples of objectives may be to detect and arrest the adversary, prevent the criminal conduct or irregularity of the adversary and create awareness to prevent losses (Garcia, 2008).

Physical protection systems

The next step in the process, if designing a new PPS, is to determine how best to combine elements such as fences, barriers, sensors, procedures, communication devices and security personnel into a PPS that can achieve the protection objectives. The resulting PPS design should meet these objectives within the operational, safety, legal and economic constraints of the facility. The primary functions of the PPS will be the detection of an adversary, delay of the adversary and response by security personnel (Garcia, 2008).

Strategies

Some situations may require immediate action and prompt intervention. Some are cyclical, managerial and are amenable to technical solutions and problem-solving methods. Others are chronic, endemic difficulties that require the application of strategies over time, to change conditions and move an organisation ahead. The security manager needs to know the differences between these, what knowledge is required and how to access it through personnel or by other means. Additionally, the security manager must explore the adequacy of the concepts from the knowledge base and how and when to apply them (Opolot, 1999). The challenge is for security managers to stay current on innovative design strategies to couple this knowledge with the latest information on issues of changes in cultural values, crime, technology, market conditions and political conditions (Opolot, 1999). Some examples of strategies may include crime prevention through environmental design (CPTED), business watch, car guard watch, neighbourhood watch, awareness, sharing of information, and electronic networking with other service providers and organisations. Many of these have served as best practices in the law enforcement environment.

Actionable crime information products

According to Peterson (1994), Goldsmith et al. (2000), and Hirschfield and Bowers (2001), actionable crime information products commonly used by law enforcement are as follows:

- case docket analysis: this is the overall study of investigation dockets to provide recommendations for its successful completion;

- activity flow charts: these are used to explain the paper trail in complex investigations, such as money laundering, commercial fraud, etc. ;

- tables: all data is placed in tabular format to ascertain any commonalities or patterns. In a series of armed robberies, for example, the factors may include: time of day, location, type of establishment robbed, number of perpetrators, use of weapons, language spoken, manner of dress of perpetrators and the type of financial instruments taken;

- matrices: these are used in analysis to organise data in such a manner that it can be compared to similar data. The triangular matrix is commonly used as an association analysis matrix. For example, with names of crimes on one side and the names of places where the crimes occur on the top side, thus connecting at a triangular point, indicating a connection or commonality;

- collection plan: this is a preliminary step towards completing a strategic assessment, which shows what needs to be collected, how it is going to be collected and by what date;

- criminal profile: this is the product of criminal investigation analysis in which indicators of behaviour and activity are used to create models. A profile is created by gathering all possible information on a type of behaviour or occurrence and then analysing and comparing that behaviour to cases or incidents on hand;

- assessments: these are a product of the strategic analysis process. They are written reports that can include the results of surveys, independent research, information gathered from independent case dockets and data received from other law enforcement sources;

- analytical briefings: these are oral presentations of findings or products based on the data analysed;

- maps: these depict the location of offences, victims and, occasionally, offenders. They can provide information concerning the location of crime hot spots or high levels of reported crimes;

- crime analysis: traditional crime analysis includes both the breaking down of criminal incidents into their composite parts (factors) to determine patterns and similarities, which may lead to the apprehension of the perpetrator(s) and also the statistical analysis of crimes to forecast future crimes. Information on a series of crimes that have been committed is used to complete a crime analysis. This information may include victim data, suspect data, dates, times and location of crimes, physical evidence, weapons used and the fruits of the crimes;

- linkage analysis: connects a suspect to one or more incidents. It can narrow search areas by identifying known criminals or other suspects who reside within a certain distance from incident locations. The objective of linkage analysis is the apprehension of suspects and case clearance;

- association analysis: depicts the relationships among people, groups, businesses or other entities in a way that provides the investigator with information on the nature of the group and the manner in which the group interacts;

- criminal investigative analysis: this entails the use of components of a crime and/or the physical and psychological attributes of a criminal, to ascertain the identity of the criminal. This technique has been used by the FBI in the area of homicide and sexually motivated crimes. Some analysts refer to it as profiling. In fact, a profile of a criminal is a product developed as a result of the criminal analysis process;

- statistical analysis: this is a review of numerical data to summarise it and to draw conclusions about its meaning;

- pie charts: these are used to give a graphic depiction of the parts of a whole; the pie equals the whole of something and the slices equal smaller parts of the whole. They are applied by law enforcement to show the occurrences of particular crimes in relation to the overall crime rate or the relative amounts/percentages of income from illegal sources. A bar chart is a graphic depiction of a certain activity in relation to or in comparison with another factor such as time, cost or another occurrence – both of which can generally be measured in numbers. It can be used in conjunction with a number of other analytical techniques;

- composite tables: all data is placed in tabular format to ascertain any commonalities or patterns. In a series of armed robberies, for example, factors may include time of day, location, type of establishment robbed, number of perpetrators, use of weapons, language spoken, manner of dress of perpetrators and the type of financial instruments taken. The information known about each of the armed robberies committed can then be put in tabular form. The table would then be reviewed for possible patterns, commonalties and differences. Conclusions about the persons responsible for the robberies can then be drawn;

- automated mapping: automated pin mapping, hot spot analysis and radial analysis are a few of the most extensively used. They can be used to identify the locations of high concentration of crimes, known as hot spots. An investigator may use intelligence and modus operandi data to identify that the same offender is likely to be responsible for a series of incidents;

- geographic flow mapping: this is a simple graphic depiction of a specific region, used to show some activity or occurrence related to criminal activity. Information gleaned from a map can relate to territories covered by a crime group or to sources and routes of goods or services being transported by crime groups;

- target profiling: this identifies locations that may have an unusually high likelihood of victimisation within an active pattern area. Within a large geographic area, offenders tend to target certain types of locations rather than others, especially for crimes influenced by the location of commercial or service-oriented activity, such as convenience stores or banks;

- offender movement pattern analysis: ties at least two or more points to one or more criminal incidents. One example is the theft location and recovery site of a stolen motor vehicle. Connecting the two locations – theft and recovery – may help identify the roads used by an offender after stealing an automobile. Similarly, relating an offender's last known residence to an arrest location, such as an open air drug market, can identify roads used by dealers to transport drugs; and

- forecasting: this is a process which predicts the future on the basis of past trends, current trends and/ or future speculations. Within the field of analysis, both numeric and descriptive forecasting are done. Numeric forecasting is numerically used and generally rests on past and current numbers of occurrences. Descriptive forecasting takes both quantitative and descriptive trend data to predict the future. Forecasting is used in both crime analysis and strategic analysis.

The abovementioned actionable crime information products may be used to reduce crime, increase detection rates and prevent losses.

Dissemination of security information analysis products

Peterson (1994) describes dissemination in the security information management process as the release of analysis products to a client, under certain conditions and protocols. It is usually based on the security classification of the information and the security clearance of the client. Jordaan (2003a) refers to dissemination as vital, as it encompasses information that was collected, analysed and which must be packaged and delivered to the clients and stakeholders who can use it. The IPA product from analysts can prompt an immediate response from the specialised anti-crime surveillance units. Taking a proactive approach is likely to reduce future incidents to be committed by the perpetrator. In a similar way, the officials may request analysts for listings of possible incidents where an arrestee may be involved. Analysts can also assist investigators with suspect and victim profiles (Reuland, 1997). Dissemination can be carried out in several different ways, namely, by attending briefings and strategy sessions, presenting verbal reports, providing written reports, having face-to-face contact whenever the need arises and public information systems for both written and electronic media (Reuland, 1997).

Feedback on security information analysis products

The last phase of the security information management process is feedback. Analysts should not go blindly forward from day to day, without knowing which output products and formats work and which do not. Analysts spend a great deal of time preparing analysis products and must know how the end users plan to use the final product and how useful it would be to them. Additionally, if the end users view the analysts' output as non-responsive to a request, they may not make additional requests. To obtain feedback, analysts should routinely include a survey form with the prepared analysis report (Reuland, 1997).

Monitoring and evaluation of security risk control measures

Monitoring and evaluation of the security risk control measures begin with the review of the security risk control measures to obtain a thorough understanding of the protection objectives the designed security risk control measures must meet. This can be done by simply checking the required features of a PPS, such as intrusion detection, entry control, access delay, response communications and response force. Crime statistics may also be used as a standard to monitor and evaluate the effectiveness of the strategies and actionable crime information products (Garcia, 2008).

CONCLUSION

This chapter that discusses the security information management process is the third part of the security information management model (SIMM). Security managers need to play a primary role in creating an environment for the security information management process to be implemented. If the process is done correctly, it will help to reduce crime, increase detection rates and prevent losses. Literature study was conducted to enhance the traditional ways of processing security information. There was limited literature in South Africa on security information management. The researcher was compelled to focus on international literature for guidance. For the model to be successful, there should be timely collection of security information on incidents, threats and vulnerabilities; rapid analysis of security information, and the prompt designing of strategies, actionable crime information products and PPS to deter, detect, delay, and respond to an adversary.

Summary

OBJECTIVES

- Understand the management of incidents, which is the consequence of vulnerabilities and threats.
- Distinguish between the concepts incidents, threats and vulnerabilities.
- Be aware of the different types of incidents and how to handle them.
- Describe the steps a security practitioner must follow when attending to security incidents.

INTRODUCTION

This book was written to enlighten security officials about security information management, which includes the collection and analysis of information on security incidents, threats and vulnerabilities and the implementation of security risk control measures. The security industry operates within a diverse and multi-disciplinary knowledge base, with security risk management being a fundamental knowledge domain within security. Over the past decade, the concept of security risk management as a formal discipline has emerged throughout the private and government sectors of security. Security risk management is now a well-established discipline, with its own body of knowledge. The standards and compliance requirements for risk management only considers security risk management and not security information management. In security risk management, security risk assessment is carried out to identify areas that need security intervention. The security risk management framework currently used by the security industry provides for security risk analysis. This does not include the day-to-day collection of security information on security incidents, threats and vulnerabilities for the purpose of reducing crime, increasing detection rates and preventing losses. In this final chapter, attention will be given to a brief summary of the kinds of security information that was discussed in this book.

SECURITY INCIDENTS, THREATS AND VULNERABILITIES

Security incidents occur because of security breaches, breaches of discipline by security officers, and poor implementation of existing security policies and procedures. Threat is considered as the consequence of the incident, which at the time the incident was taking place, may have affected people, information or assets. In the security context, a threat may be defined as an adversary, being the sum of intent and capability (Smith and Brooks, 2013). Vulnerability on the other hand gives exposure for an incident to occur, causing physical and emotional hurt, being open to attack, or lacking resilience (Smith and Brooks, 2013). It was found that in many organisations/ companies security incidents are managed without any strategic direction and infrastructure. Security incident information is collected using specific personnel and electronic technology whenever an incident takes place. The most common sources from which security incident information is collected include information from a victim/complainant and witnesses. Volunteered incident information is sometimes received from a third party on specific incidents. Security incident information received by security officials is recorded in the security official's pocket book/diary and then transferred into an incident register called the "Occurrence book," which is usually kept in the operations control room. In some cases, the incident information is entered into a computer system in the control room. Procedurally the control room supervisor/manager takes note of the incident.

The security information on incidents of crime is handed to the South African Police Service (SAPS) for the opening of a police case docket as a prelude to the incident's criminal investigation and for possible criminal proceedings being instituted. Incident information on violations of company policy and security breaches, breaches of discipline by security officers, and lax implementation of existing security policies and procedures are handled by the control room supervisors. The police attend to the criminal incident and gives the security official/complainant/victim a case number for every crime incident registered for investigation, which is recorded in the occurrence book in the control room. SAPS investigates the incident for the purpose of tracing offenders and ensuring prosecution. If it is a criminal incident, the in-house security response team also attends to the incident. In incidents of popular interest, the supervisor on duty in the control room visits the scene of the incident to ascertain the nature and gravity of the incident. When crime incidents are reported to SAPS, it is also recorded in the crime administration system (CAS) of SAPS for statistical purposes and analysis. This information is subsequently used to enrich the crime pattern analysis (CPA) document for use by police officials in their day-to-day operations.

In big organisations/companies all incidents of violations of company policy and security breaches, breaches of discipline by security officers, and lax implementation of existing security policies and procedures are handled internally by the human resources department and the crime information is handled by the intelligence/ information unit or the in-house investigation unit.

It is essential that all personnel know where, how and to whom to report the security incidents. If there is confusion, serious security incidents may go unreported or inadequately managed. As soon as an incident has been confirmed and the security incident response team (SIRT) has been informed, it should be documented in an incident register (Wilding, 2006). An incident register is used to identify incidents related to threats. The incident register will consist of reported incidents experienced by the organisation and information on who, what, when, where, why and how of each, action taken as the incident unfolded (Jacobs, Shepherd, and Johnson, 1998). The incident register report should serve as a case study after the fact to determine if the right actions were taken and if they were effective. Such a case study can also be used as a stimulation in future training sessions (Whitman and Mattord, 2008; Curtis and McBride, 2011). The recorded incidents should be used to enrich the threat assessment document of the organisation/company (Talbot and Jakeman, 2008). All security incidents that take place in an organisation/company should be subject to investigation by the organisation/company where the incident took place (Talbot and Jakeman, 2008).

There are three most common types of incidents that confront organisations that are being protected. The first one is where security practitioners have to deal with incidents that have happened and the culprits are known (Wilding, 2006). If the security officer is responding to such an incident in the workplace, where the incident has already taken place, and where the identity of the suspect is known, the priority will be to safeguard all the available evidence as quickly as possible in order to prevent it from being tampered with, overlooked or lost, either intentionally or otherwise. Under these circumstances, the crime scene needs to be secured. All loopholes need to be identified and closed. Searches should be conducted lawfully and with due regard to decency. A decision has to be made as soon as possible as to whether the police should be called in. If the police do attend and commence with the investigation, then all operational decisions will pass through them. If it is decided that an internal enquiry should be conducted, it may be necessary to call upon the internal investigation unit or external specialists to assist with the investigation or to review particular systems or processes.

The second type of incident where the culprit is unknown often happens in the workplace. The third type is where information comes from a reliable source of a likely incident taking place in the organisation/company sometime in the future, which is bound to negatively affect the assets of the organisation. Under these circumstances, a corporate investigation should be immediately instituted. The collection of information for the investigation of crime must be conducted in a lawful way, so that the evidence can indeed be admissible as evidence. The evidence must also be of such a nature that the unlawful act of the accused is demonstrated beyond any reasonable doubt. For this reason, systematic and planned action is an essential part of criminal investigation (Van Heerden, 1986). It is important to ensure the integrity of information that has been collected. This will avoid legal restrictions that may prevent the introduction of such information as evidence at a trial or the development of a solid case for prosecution (Gardner, 2005). Information collected during workplace investigations may enlighten management on the extent of incidents in the organisation. Investigations of security incidents or events are conducted for a number of other purposes, namely civil proceedings for damages for loss sustained during a security attack; internal disciplinary proceedings; a post-event internal review of security and response procedures; or compliance with policy or the law. Many security incidents necessarily result in either criminal or civil proceedings. The incident may be no more than an employee's violation of company policy, such as the improper use of the network computer to access the internet or an employee's entry to the company's facility without scanning an identification card or sleeping on duty (Curtis and McBride, 2011).

CONCLUSION

Incidents, threats and vulnerabilities have the potential to affect an organisation's assets negatively. Information on these incidents, threats and vulnerabilities are important to security. It is therefore necessary for this security information to be managed effectively and efficiently, so that correct decisions can be made on the implementation of security risk control measures. This book explored the management of security information in the security industry by undertaking the following:

- establishing the security information practices both in South Africa and Western Australia;

- identifying the nature and extent of problems experienced in the collection and analysis of security information and the implementation of security risk control measures; and

- recommending a security information management model (SIMM).

The grounded theory design was used to research the management of security information in the security industry in both South Africa and Australia. The explorative research design was useful in obtaining grounded data. Semi-structured and focus group interviews were conducted with senior security managers and operational security officers, respectively. The grounded theory research design was also used to analyse the qualitative data in order to generate a substantive grounded theory.

The study found that there was a need for a SIMM to manage security information in the security industry. Based on this theory the researcher recommended a new SIMM for the management of security information in the security industry.

Bibliography

PUBLISHED SOURCES

Abrie, S. 2008. *Security Risk Management*. University of South Africa Study Guide for PSMN03X. Pretoria: University of South Africa.

Ainsworth, P. B. 2001. *Offender Profiling and Crime Analysis*. Portland, OR: Willan.

Allen, R. E. (ed). 1992. *Concise Oxford Dictionary*. 8th edition. Oxford: Clarendon Press.

Altbeker, A. 1998. *Solving Crime: The State of the SAPS Detective Service*. ISS Monograph No. 31. Pretoria: Institute for Security Studies. Available at: http://www.iss.co.za/pgcontent.php?UID=1587.

Atkin, H. 2000. Criminal Intelligence Analysis: A Scientific Perspective. *Journal of Intelligence and Analysis*, 13(1), May: 3–7.

Australian Security Industry Association Ltd. (ASIAL). 2011. *Who Should Hold a Security Licence?* Available at: http://www.asial.com.au/. (Accessed 9 August 2011).

Bernstein, P. L. 1996. *Against the Gods: The Remarkable Story of Risk*, New York: John Wiley and Sons.

Block, C., Dabdoub, M., and Fregly, S. 1995. *Crime Analysis Through Computer Mapping*. Washington, DC: Police Executive Research Forum.

Blyth, A. and Kovacich, G. L. 2006. *Information Assurance: Security in the Information Environment*. Second edition. USA: Springer.

Bosch, J. G. S. 1999. *The Role of Structure of the Private Security Industry in South Africa*. ISSUP Bulletin. Pretoria.

Bozza, C. M. 1978. *Criminal Investigation*. Chicago: Nelson Hall.

Broder, J. F. 2000. *Risk Analysis and the Security Survey*. Oxford: Butterworth-Heinemann.

Bureau of Justice Assistance, 2013. *Compstat. Its Origins, Evolution and Future in Law Enforcement Agencies*. Washington DC: Police Executive Research Forum.

Burt, V. 2004. *Test Your Management Skills*. London: Hodder and Stoughton.

Clark, R. 2010. *Intelligence Analysis: A Target-centric Approach*. 3rd edition. Washington: CQ press.

Clarke, R. V. and Eck, J. 2003. *Become a Problem-solving Crime Analyst in 55 Small Steps*. London: Jill Dando Institute of Crime Science, University College.

Curtis, G. E. and McBride, R. B. 2011. *Proactive Security Administration*. 2nd edition. Upper Saddle River: Prentice Hall.

DefenceWeb. 2011. New Law to Fix Security Industry Gaps: Mthethwa (Speech given at Annual Conference of the Security Industry Alliance by Minister of Police, Nathi

Mthethwa, on 15 November). Available at http://www.defenceweb.co.za/index.php?option=com_content&task=view&id=21125&catid=3&Itemid=113

Du Preez, G. T. 1996. *Forensic Criminalistics: Criminal Investigation.* 2nd edition, Pretoria: University of South Africa.

Edwards, C. 2011. *Changing Policing Theories for 21st-Century Societies.* 3rd edition. Sydney: The Federation Press.

Ekblom, P. 1988. *Getting the Best out of Crime Analysis.* London: Crown.

Fay, J. J. 2006. *Contemporary Security Management.* Oxford: Butterworth-Heinemann.

Ferraro, E. F. and Spain, N. M. 2006. *Investigations in the Workplace.* New York: Auerbach.

Fennelly, L. J. 2004. *Effective Physical Security.* Oxford: Butterworth-Heinemann.

Fischer, R. J., Halibozeck, E. and Green, G. 2008. *Introduction to security.* 8th edition. Oxford: Butterworth-Heinemann.

Fischer, B. A. J. 2004. *Techniques of Crime Investigation.* 7th edition. Washington, DC: CRC.

Garcia, M. L. 2001. *The Design and Evaluation of Physical Protection Systems.* Oxford: Butterworth-Heinemann.

Garcia, M. L. 2006. *Vulnerability Assessment of Physical Protection Systems.* Oxford: Butterworth-Heinemann.

Garcia, M. L. 2008. *The Design and Evaluation of Physical Protection Systems.* 2nd edition. Oxford: Butterworth-Heinemann. https://doi.org/10.1016/B978-0-08-055428-0.50005-1

Gardner, R. M. 2005. Practical Crime Scene Processing and Investigation: Practical Aspects of Criminal and Forensic Investigation Series. Washington, DC: CRC Press.

Goldsmith, V., McGuire, P. G., Mollenkopf, J. H. and Ross, T. A. 2000. *Analysing Crime Patterns: Frontiers of Practice.* Thousand Oaks, CA: Sage.

Gottlieb, S., Arenberg, S. and Singh, R. 1994. *Crime Analysis: From First Report to Final Arrest.* Montclair, CA: Alpha.

Gumedze, S. 2015. *Promoting Partnerships for Crime Prevention between State and Private Security Providers in South Africa.* Private Security Industry Regulatory Authority, Pretoria: PSIRA.

Hirschfield, A. and Bowers, K. 2001. *Mapping and Analysing Crime Data: Lessons from Research and Practice.* London: Taylor and Francis.

Horne, J. S. 2009. Crime Information Analysis within a Public Service Organisation: An Assessment. *Acta Criminologica: Southern African Journal of Criminology,* 22(1):68–80.

Irish, J. 1999. *Policing for profit: The future of South Africa's private security industry.* ISS Monograph No. 39. Pretoria: Institute for Security Studies.

Jacobs, T., Shepherd, J. and Johnson, G. 1998. Strengths, Weaknesses, Opportunities and Threats (SWOT) Analysis. Pp. 122–138. In Ambrosini, V. Johnson, G. and Scholes, K. 1998. *Exploring Techniques of Analysis and Evaluation in Strategic Management.* Upper Saddle River, NJ: Prentice Hall.

Johnson, B. R. 2005. *Principles of security management.* Upper Saddle River, NJ: Prentice Hall.

Jones, T. and Newburn, T. 2006. *Plural Policing: A comparative perspective*. London: Routledge.

Jordaan, J. 2003a. The Role of Intelligence in Investigations (Part 1). *Servamus*, 96(4), April: 56–59.

Jordaan, J. 2003b. The Role of Intelligence in Investigations (Part 2). *Servamus*, 96(5), May: 58–59.

Kelling, G. L., Pate, A. M., Dieckman, D., and Brown, C. 1974. *The Kansas City Preventive Patrol Experiment: Technical Report*. Washington, DC: Police Foundation.

King, M. E. 1994. *The King Report on Corporate Governance*. Parklands: Institute of Directors in South Africa.

Kritzinger, E. 2006. An Information Security Retrieval and Awareness Model for Industry. PhD thesis. University of South Africa, Pretoria.

Leitch, M. 2010. Risk Management Model ISO 31000:2009, The New International Standard on Risk Management, *Risk Analysis*, 30(6).

Le Roux, G. J. 2004. A Quantitative Risk Analysis Model for Private Security Managers. DLit et Phil thesis, University of South Africa, Pretoria.

Louw, A. 2001. Understanding Police Crime Statistics. *Crime Index South Africa*, 5(3), May/June: 1–5.

Lyman, M. D. 1988. *Criminal Investigation: The Art and the Science*. Upper Saddle River, NJ: Prentice Hall.

MacHovec, F. 2006. *Private Investigation and Security Science: A Scientific Approach*. Springfield, IL: Charles C. Thomas Publishing.

Marais, C.W. and Van Rooyen, H. J. N. 1990. *Misdaadondersoek*. Silverton: Promedia Publications.

Matthews, A. 1986. Freedom, State Security and the Rule of Law: Dilemmas of Apartheid Society. Cape Town: Juta.

Minister for Safety and Security. 2007. *Nqakula: Safety and Security Dept Budget Vote 2007/08*. Available at http://www.polity.org.za/article/nqakula-safety-and-security-dept-budget-vote-200708-22052007-2007-05-22.

Minnaar, A. 2005. Private-Public Partnerships: Private Security, Crime Prevention and Policing in South Africa, *Acta Criminologica: Southern African Journal of Criminology*, 18(1): 85–114.

Minnaar, A. 2007. A Review of the Issues and Challenges Facing the Private Security Industry in South Africa. Unpublished research report. Pretoria: Department of Security Risk Management, University of South Africa/Open Society Foundation.

Minnaar, A. and Nogoveni, P. 2004. The relationship between the South African Police Service and the private security industry: Any role for outsourcing in the prevention of crime? *Acta Criminologica: Southern African Journal of Criminology*, 17(1): 42–65.

Montgomery, R. J. and Majeski, W. J. 2005. *Corporate Investigations*. 2nd edition. Tucson, AZ: Lawyers and Judges Publishing Company.

Muller, M. L. 2002a. *Defending Against Hostile Competitive Intelligence. A Practical Guide for Leaders* (Guide 2. Nuts and Bolts Business Series/Competitive Intelligence

Series). Randburg: Knowledge Resources.

Muller, M. L. 2002b. *Gathering Competitive Information. A Practical Guide for Leaders* (Guide 3. Nuts and Bolts Business Series/Competitive Intelligence Series). Randburg: Knowledge Resources.

Muller, M. L. 2002c. *Creating Intelligence. A Practical Guide for Leaders* (Guide 4. Nuts and Bolts Business Series/Competitive Intelligence Series). Randburg: Knowledge Resources.

Muller, M. L. and Whitehead, C. 2002. *What is Competitive Intelligence? A Practical Guide for Leaders* (Guide 1. Nuts and Bolts Business Series/Competitive Intelligence Series). Randburg: Knowledge Resources.

National Criminal Intelligence Service (NCIS). 2000. *The National Intelligence Model.* London: Home Office, National Criminal Intelligence Service.

Nemeth, C. P. 2010. *Private Security and the Investigative Process.* 3rd edition. New York: Auerbach. https://doi.org/10.1201/b11550

Newburn, T., Williamson, T. and Wright, A. 2008. *Handbook of Criminal Investigation.* Cullompton: Willan.

O'Block, R. L. 1981. *Security and Crime Prevention.* St Louis, MO: C. V. Mosby.

Opolot, J. S. E. 1999. *An Introduction to Private Security: A Comparative Introduction to an International Phenomenon.* New York: Austin and Winfield.

Paulsen, D. J. 2004. To Map or Not To Map: Assessing the Impact of Crime Maps on Police Officer Perceptions of Crime. *International Journal of Police Science and Management,* 6(4), August: 234–246. https://doi.org/10.1350/ijps.6.4.234.54136

Peterson, M. B. 1994. *Applications in criminal analysis: A sourcebook.* Westport, CT: Greenwood Press.

Post, R. S. and Kingsbury, A. A. 1991. *Security Administration: An Introduction to the Protection Services.* 4th edition. Oxford: Butterworth-Heinemann.

Prenzler, T., Earle, K. and Sarre, R. 2009. *Private Security in Australia: Trends and Key Characteristics.* Trends and Issues in Crime and Criminal Justice, No. 374. Canberra: Australian Institute of Criminology.

Private Security Regulatory Authority. 2012. *Private Security Industry in South Africa.* Available at: www.psira.sa.co.za. (Accessed 10 February 2012).

Pupura, P. P. 2013. *Security and Loss Prevention. An Introduction.* 6th edition. Oxford: Butterworth-Heinemann.

Ratcliffe, J. H. 2003. *Intelligence-Led Policing.* Trends and Issues in Crime and Criminal Justice, No. 248. Canberra: Australian Institute of Criminology.

Ratcliffe, J. 2009. *Intelligence-Led Policing.* Portland, OR: Willan.

Redpath, J. 2004. *The Scorpions: Analysing the Directorate of Special Operations. Justice in Action.* ISS Monograph No. 96. Pretoria: Institute for Security Studies.

Reuland, M. M. 1997. *Information Management and Crime Analysis.* Washington, DC: Police Executive Research Forum.

Ribaux, O., Girod, A., Walsh, S., Margot, P., Mizrahi, S. and Clivaz, C. 2003. *Forensic Intelligence and Crime Analysis, Law, Probability and Risk.* Washington, DC: CRC Press.

Rogers, C. 2008. A Security Risk Management Approach to the Measurement of Crime in a Private Security Context. *Acta Criminologica. Southern African Journal of Criminology*. Crimsa 2008 Conference Special Edition (3) 2008. 150–156.

Shaw, G. 2002. Effective Security Analysis. *IT-Security journal*. April 2002.

Sherman, L. and Weisburd, D. 1995. General Deterrent Effects of Police Patrol in Crime "Hot Spots": A Randomised, Controlled Trial. *Justice Quarterly*, 12(4), 625–648. https://doi.org/10.1080/07418829500096221

Simonsen, C. E. 1998. *Private Security in America: An Introduction*. Upper Saddle River, NJ: Prentice Hall.

Smit, P. J. and Cronjé, G. J. de J. 2002. *Management Principles: A Contemporary Edition for Africa*. Cape Town: Juta.

Smit, B. F. 1989. *Police Science*: Study guide for POL 203–P (Security). Pretoria: University of South Africa.

Smith, P. and Natalier, K. 2005. *Understanding Criminal Justice: Sociological Perspectives*. London: Sage.

Smith, C. L. and Brooks, D. J. 2013. *Security Science: The Theory and Practice of Security*. Oxford: Butterworth-Heinemann.

South African Banking Risk Information Centre (SABRIC). 2011. Business presentation at Midrand SAPS 10111 centre. Available at: https://www.sabric.co.za. (Accessed 7 June 2011).

Stelfox, P. 2009. *Criminal Investigations: An Introduction to Principles and Practice*. Cullompton: Willan.

Talbot, J. and Jakeman, M. 2009. *Security Risk Management: Body of Knowledge (SRMBOK)*. Hoboken, NJ: Wiley-Blackwell.

Tilley, N. 2009. *Crime Prevention*. Cullompton: Willan.

Valsamakis, A. C., Vivian, R. W. and Du Toit, G. S. 1996. *The Theory and Principles of Risk Management*. Johannesburg: Heinemann.

Van Heerden, T. J. 1986. *Inleiding tot die Polisiekunde*. Pretoria: University of South Africa.

Van Rooyen, H. J. N. 2008. *The Practitioner's Guide to Forensic Investigation in South Africa*. Pretoria: Henmar Publications.

Whitman, M. E. and Mattord, H. J. 2008. *Management of Information Security*. 2nd edition. Course Technology. Boston, MA: Gex.

Wilding. E. 2006. *Information Risk and Security: Preventing and Investigating Workplace Computed Crime*. Aldershot: Gower.

Zedner, L. 2003. The Concept of Security: An Agenda for Comparative Analysis. *Legal Studies*, 23(1): 153. https://doi.org/10.1111/j.1748-121X.2003.tb00209.x

ACTS

South Africa. 1977. Criminal Procedures Act 51 of 1977. *Government Gazette* 5827. Pretoria: Government Printer. 27 December.

South Africa. 1980. National Key Points Act 102 of 1980. Pretoria: Government Printer.

South Africa. 1982. Protection of Information Act 84 of 1982. Pretoria: Government Printer.

South Africa. 1987. South African Security Officer's Act 92 of 1987. Pretoria: Government Printer.

South Africa. 1992. Interception and Monitoring Act 127 of 1992. Pretoria: Government Printer.

South Africa. 1994. National Strategic Intelligence Act 39 of 1994. *Government Gazette* 16128. Pretoria: Government Printer. 2 December.

South Africa. 1995. South African Police Service Act 68 of 1995. *Government Gazette* 16731. Pretoria: Government Printer. 6 October.

South Africa. 1996. The Constitution of the Republic of South Africa 108 of 1996. *Government Gazette* 17678. Pretoria: Government Printer. 18 December.

South Africa. 2000a. Promotion of Access to Information Act 2 of 2000. *Government Gazette* 20852. Pretoria: Government Printer. 3 February.

South Africa. 2000b. Protected Disclosures Act 26 of 2000. *Government Gazette* 21453. Pretoria: Government Printer. 7 August.

South Africa. 2001. Private Security Industry Regulatory Act 56 of 2001. *Government Gazette* 23051. Pretoria: Government Printer. 25 January.

South Africa 2013. Protection of Personal Information Act 4 of 2013.

Government Gazette 37067. Pretoria: Government Printer. 26 November

INTERVIEWS

Australian Government official. 2011a. Head of Security of a government department. Confidential interview with author. 26 May. Perth, Western Australia.

Australian Government official. 2011b. Head of Security of a government department. Confidential interview with author. 26 May. Perth, Western Australia.

Australian Police Officer. 2011a. Investigation and Enforcement Head of a government department. Confidential interview with author. 18 May. Perth, Western Australia.

Australian Police Officer. 2011b. Senior police official from the WA Police. Confidential interview with author. 10 May. Perth, Western Australia.

Australian Police Officer. 2011c. Senior police official from the WA Police. Confidential interview with author. 13 May. Perth, Western Australia.

Australian Academic. 2011a. Senior academic from ECU. School of computing and security science. Confidential interview with author. 17 May. Perth, Western Australia.

Australian Academic. 2011b. Senior academic from ECU: School of computing and security science. Confidential interview with author. 17 May. Perth, Western Australia.

Australian Academic. 2011c. Senior academic from ECU: School of computing and security science. Confidential interview with author. 23 May. Perth, Western Australia.

Australian Academic. 2011d. Senior academic from ECU: School of computing and security science. Confidential interview with author. 24 May. Perth, Western Australia.

Australian Academic. 2011e. Associate Research Professor from ECU: School of computing and security science. Confidential interview with author. 13 May. Perth, Western Australia.

Australian Security Service Provider. 2011a. Director of a contract security service provider (commercial/residential security). Confidential interview with author. 18 May. Perth, Western Australia.

Australian Security Service Provider. 2011b. Security manager of a contract security service provider (banking security). Confidential interview with author. 19 May. Perth, Western Australia.

Australian Security Service Provider. 2011c. Security adviser of a contract security service provider (mining security). Confidential interview with author. 23 May. Perth, Western Australia.

Australian Security Service Provider. 2011d. Security manager of an in-house security service provider (campus security). Confidential interview with author. 23 May. Perth, Western Australia.

Australian Security Service Provider. 2011e. Security manager of an in-house security service provider (casino security). Confidential interview with author. 25 May. Perth, Western Australia.

Australian Security Service Provider. 2011f. Security manager of an in-house security service provider (casino security). Confidential interview with author. 25 May. Perth, Western Australia.

Australian Security Service Provider. 2011g. Director of a contract security service provider (industrial security). Confidential interview with author. 18 May. Perth, Western Australia.

Conradie, S. 2010. CEO of Security Industry Alliance. Interview with author. 18 November. Johannesburg, Gauteng, South Africa.

CGRI. 2010. Senior managers from CGRI. Confidential interview with author. 22 June. Johannesburg, Gauteng, South Africa.

De Kock, C. 2011. Deputy Divisional Commissioner, SAPS Crime Intelligence Division. Interview with author. 14 January. Pretoria, Gauteng, South Africa

Maree, A. 2010. Senior Manager, Violent Crime Office SABRIC. Interview with author. 25 June. Johannesburg, Gauteng, South Africa.

PSI. 2010. Senior managers from . Confidential interview with author. 6 July. Pretoria, Gauteng South Africa.

Reddy, O. D. 2010. Assistant Commissioner, SAPS Honeydew Cluster Commander. Interview with author. 5 March. Johannesburg, Gauteng, South Africa

SABRIC. 2010. Senior manager, Violent Crime Office. SABRIC. Confidential interview with author. 16 April. Johannesburg, Gauteng, South Africa.

South African Government official 2010a. Senior security officer from a government department. Confidential interview with author. 8 April. Johannesburg, Gauteng, South Africa.

South African Government official 2010b. Senior security officer from a government department. Confidential interview with author. 20 April. Pretoria, Gauteng, South Africa.

South African Police Officer. 2011. Crime Intelligence officer. Confidential interview with author. 11 March, Pretoria, Gauteng, South Africa.

South African Security Service Provider. 2010a. Security manager of a contract security service provider. Confidential interview with author. 11 May. Pretoria, Gauteng, South Africa.

South African Security Service Provider. 2010b. Security manager of an in-house security service provider (complex security). Confidential interview with author. 19 March. Pretoria, Gauteng, South Africa.

South African Security Service Provider. 2010c. Security manager of an in-house security service provider (petroleum company). Confidential interview with author. 23 March. Johannesburg, Gauteng, South Africa.

South African Security Service Provider. 2010d. Security manager of an in-house security service provider (banking security). Confidential interview with author. 8 July. Johannesburg, Gauteng, South Africa.

South African Security Service Provider. 2010e. Security manager of an in-house security service provider (campus security). Confidential interview with author. 9 April. Pretoria, Gauteng, South Africa.

South African Security Service Provider. 2010f. Security manager of an in-house security service provider (retail security). Confidential interview with author. 15 April. Pretoria, Gauteng, South Africa.

South African Security Service Provider. 2010g. Security manager of an in-house security service provider (mining security). Confidential interview with author. 24 March. Johannesburg, Gauteng, South Africa.

South African Security Service Provider. 2010h. Security manager of an in-house security service provider (casino security). Confidential interview with author. 21 April. Johannesburg, Gauteng, South Africa.

South African Security Service Provider. 2010i. CEO of a contract security service provider. Confidential interview with author. 29 April. Pretoria, Gauteng, South Africa.

South African Security Service Provider. 2010j. CEO of an in-house security service provider (mining security). Confidential interview with author. 24 March. Johannesburg, Gauteng, South Africa.

South African Security Service Provider. 2010k. CEO of a contract security service provider (residential Security). Confidential interview with author. 6 December. Pretoria, Gauteng, South Africa.

South African Security Service Provider. 2010l. Investigator of a contract security service provider (insurance investigations). Confidential interview with author. 19 May. Johannesburg, Gauteng, South Africa.

South African Security Service Provider. 2010m. Security manager of a contract security service provider (retail security). Confidential interview with author. 22 June. Johannesburg, Gauteng, South Africa.

South African Security Service Provider. 2010n. Security manager of an in-house security service provider (campus security). 2010. Confidential interview with author. 15 March. Pretoria, Gauteng, South Africa.

South African Academic. 2011. Senior academic from University of South Africa. Department of Criminology and Security Science, Programme Security Management. Confidential interview with author. 15 March. Pretoria, Gauteng, South Africa.

Index